SCHOOL COUNSELING: THE PATH TO SUCCESS

WLADIMIR LEWIS-THOMAS, PH.D.

ISBN 978-1-969201-88-2

Dedication

This work is dedicated to the school counselors—past and present—of Community School Districts 17, 18, 22, 24, 25, and 28.

Special recognition is given to Eric Ward, Dr. Evelyn W. Castro, Ernest Logan, Rubain Dorancy, Esq., Sheena Buie, and Caesar Melgarejo, whose guidance, mentorship, and unwavering commitment to student success have greatly influenced my understanding of the revolutionary power of school counseling.

Their leadership and dedication have proven how counseling extends far beyond academic support, shaping the holistic growth and lifelong well-being of every student. This work would not have been possible without their inspiration and example.

Contents

Author's Note

The question, "What does a school counselor do?" is one that professionals in the field hear far too often. For those of us who have dedicated our careers to school counseling, this lack of understanding can be frustrating. The reality is that school counselors play a vital role in shaping students' academic, social, and emotional success—yet their contributions are frequently overlooked or misunderstood.

Throughout my career as a licensed school counselor, I have observed a persistent gap in how counseling is perceived within the educational system. While counselors receive extensive training in psychology and counseling techniques, the connection between these skills and academic achievement is often underappreciated. This disconnect is especially evident in middle schools, where counselors face the challenge of helping students navigate critical developmental stages while also supporting their academic progress.

The purpose of this book is to bridge that gap. It offers a clear rationale for why comprehensive school counseling programs are essential and why every school should be served by a qualified, licensed counselor. By exploring the intersection of mental health, personal development, and academic success, this book aims to demonstrate that counseling is not an optional service—it is a cornerstone of effective education.

In the chapters that follow, you will gain insight into the multifaceted role of school counselors, the strategies they employ to foster student growth, and the measurable impact they have on school communities. My hope is that this work will not only inform educators and policymakers but also empower counselors to advocate for their profession with confidence and clarity.

Introduction

I had never planned to become a school counselor. In fact, if someone had told me years ago that I would dedicate my career to this field, I would have been surprised. My foray into school counseling was unexpected, but it turned out to be one of the most fulfilling paths I could have taken.

New York City, where I live, has one of the largest school systems in the country. It also has one of the highest numbers of school counselors. Even with that, many schools still do not have enough counselors to meet the needs of their students. The role of a school counselor is crucial, yet often misunderstood or undervalued. Through my experiences, I have seen firsthand the impact that effective counseling can have on students, families, and schools.

My passion for school counseling is rooted not only in my professional experiences but also in my journey as a student making my way through a new and unfamiliar education system.

I came to the United States from Haiti when I was just 8 years old. I was placed in a public school and assigned to a bilingual Spanish-speaking classroom, where the teacher spoke both English and Spanish, but I only spoke Haitian Creole. I was the only Haitian student in the class, and I felt completely lost. I couldn't understand anything that was being said, and I often felt isolated and confused.

It was then that I knew that I had to work hard to learn English, and nothing would get in my way. Over time, I was able to adjust and understand more and more each day. By the time I was ready for sixth grade, I was reading English at a level two years above my grade. That progress gave me a surge of confidence and helped me discover a love for learning.

In the seventh grade, I was introduced to psychology for the first time, and I became fascinated by how the human mind operates. That class helped me understand some of the feelings I had as a new immigrant and made me more interested in how people grow, change, and behave. From that moment on, I knew I wanted to learn more about human development.

When it was time for high school, I chose to attend Edward R. Murrow High School in Brooklyn, New York, because it offered psychology classes to students. That decision greatly impacted the path I would take in life. After high school, I went on to Brooklyn College and majored in psychology. While there, I met Dr. Peter Weston, who became my mentor. He was the first and only person of color in the psychology department at the time. He believed in me and encouraged me to pursue graduate school to further my studies in counseling.

At first, I planned to become a therapist. But when I began graduate studies at Teachers College, Columbia University, I changed direction. I saw a greater need in schools, especially in the public school system. That led me to school counseling. As I began working in schools, I saw how important it was to use research and best practices to truly support students.

Eventually, I became a Supervisor of Guidance. During that time, I also earned my Ph.D. in Educational Counseling. My dissertation focused on "Identity Formation in Adolescent African-American Males." I chose this topic because I had spent years working with this population and saw firsthand the many challenges they faced in school and in life.

Over time, I took on a leadership role as an Assistant Principal, eventually becoming an administrator in school counseling. This position gave me a broader perspective on the profession, allowing me to see both the strengths and the gaps in the system. I realized that while personal experience was valuable, research and data-driven approaches were equally important. My work has always balanced these two aspects: what I have seen and learned in practice, and what research tells us about effective counseling strategies.

Even after retiring as an administrator, my dedication to this profession did not end. I have continued to teach at the graduate level, training new generations of school counselors. My goal is to prepare them not just for the realities of the job but also for the evolving needs of students in today's world.

From being a lost immigrant child to an educational leader, I've learned how powerful school counselors can be in shaping the lives of students. I want all school counselors to understand who their students are, what shapes them, and how we can serve as a bridge to their success. We have the tools to help them grow, not just academically, but emotionally and socially as well.

As I moved through different levels, from elementary to middle and to high school, I gained a clearer understanding of how essential school counseling is in shaping student success across the developmental lifespan.

This book reflects my journey, my experiences, and the lessons I have learned. It is also a guide for current and future school counselors who want to make a meaningful difference. By combining personal insights with research-based strategies, I hope to provide valuable knowledge that can help strengthen the field of school counseling.

In the chapters ahead, I will explore the evolution of school counseling, its role in education, and the challenges counselors face. I will discuss the skills and strategies that can make school counselors more effective, and I will highlight the importance of advocacy in ensuring that every student has access to the support they need.

School counseling is more than a job; it is a calling. It requires dedication, compassion, and a commitment to helping students navigate their academic and personal lives. My hope is that this book will inspire and equip counselors with the tools they need to succeed in this important work. It will also serve as a guide for school administrators with limited knowledge or background in school counseling. And counseling is often misunderstood. Many people, including teachers, parents, and even students, are unsure about what a school counselor *actually* does. Some think we only help with college applications, providing students and caregivers with articulation applications from one level to the next, while others believe we are just there for students in crisis. In truth, it is far more complex.

I spent 32 years in the public school system, working in over 200 schools across many school districts in the largest city in the United States, New York City. Every day, I encountered students who had no stable home, no parents available to guide them, and no clear path forward. Some had experienced trauma beyond what most adults could imagine. Many turned to social media and technology to escape their reality, but that escape did not provide them with the tools to overcome their difficulties.

One of the most important messages I share with students is this: Success is possible. You can make possible what appears to be impossible. It does not matter where you come from or how little you have—if you are willing to work hard, set goals, and take small steps toward them, you can achieve your dreams. I know this because I lived it. When I speak to young people, I tell them that the success they see in me did not come easily. It was built through effort, discipline, and a belief that I could shape my future.

As school counselors, we must be the ones to help students see these possibilities. But to do that, we need the right skills, resources, and strategies. We cannot rely on instinct alone and require data, assessment tools, and research-backed programs to guide our work. We also need to understand our identity as school counselors. What exactly do we do? How do we help students when we do not teach in the classroom? How do we create meaningful change when we only see a student for a short time each day?

These are the questions I will explore in this book. By sharing my experiences, the lessons I have learned, and the research that supports effective school counseling, I hope to provide guidance for both new and experienced professionals. School counseling is not just a job—it is a mission. And when done well, it can change lives.

Many students today are living in a world that is not entirely real. Social media, the internet, and technology have created a space where everything is filtered, edited, and curated to appear perfect. Young people spend hours online, scrolling through images and videos that show an idealized version of life—one that rarely reflects the struggles, setbacks, or challenges that come with reality.

This has serious consequences. When real-life problems occur—whether it's failure, rejection, or disappointment—many students struggle to cope. They have unrealistic expectations about success, relationships, and personal achievement. They expect immediate results because that is what they see online. They believe that life should be easy, that success should come quickly, and that happiness is constant. When reality does not match these expectations, the result is frustration, anxiety, and sometimes even depression.

As a society, we are not addressing this issue the way we should. Schools, families, and communities need to take a closer look at how technology is shaping the mindset of young people. This is especially important for school counselors. We must help students develop the skills they need to face real-world challenges.

One of the greatest struggles I have encountered in my career is training future school counselors—and even those already working in the field—to use data in their work. Many counselors are uncomfortable with data. They do not always know how to collect, analyze, and apply it to counseling interventions. But data is essential. It allows us to assess the needs of students, track progress, and identify effective methods for addressing social, emotional, and academic concerns.

Without the right guidance and professional supervision, school counselors can find themselves working without direction. They may offer support based on intuition rather than concrete evidence of what students need. This can lead to missed opportunities for real impact.

As counselors, we need to ask:

- How can we help students build resilience in a world that promotes instant gratification?

- How can we teach them to set realistic goals and take small, consistent steps toward success?

- How can we prepare them for adulthood, where they will need to manage responsibilities like paying bills, maintaining a job, and handling setbacks?

These are critical questions. If we fail to address them, we risk allowing an entire generation to grow up without the problem-solving skills, emotional strength, and work ethic needed to succeed in life. It is our responsibility as school counselors to bridge this gap between illusion and reality. We must equip students with the tools they need to navigate the real world—not just the one they see online.

The Role and Identity of School Counselors

One of the biggest challenges in school counseling is defining our role. Even today, people constantly ask, *What exactly do school counselors do?* The lack of clarity about our purpose has been an ongoing struggle.

School counselors are in the minority within the school system. The focus in education has always been on instruction—teaching subjects like math, science, and reading. And that focus is important. But we cannot ignore the fact that academic success is deeply connected to social and emotional well-being. A student dealing with anxiety, grief, or family problems will not perform well in the classroom. A student without guidance or direction may not see the point of education at all.

This is where school counselors come in. We bridge the gap between academic instruction and social-emotional development. We help students build confidence, the ability to bounce back after getting knocked down, and problem-solving skills—traits that are just as important as good grades when it comes to future success. Despite that, many schools still treat counseling as something extra, something that happens only when a student is in crisis. This mindset must change.

In many schools, especially in urban areas, there is often only one counselor for hundreds of students. That counselor is expected to provide academic guidance, emotional support, and crisis intervention—while also advocating for the profession itself. It can be overwhelming. Teachers, who make up the majority of school staff, naturally focus on instruction. They are under pressure to meet academic goals, prepare students for tests, and manage their classrooms. But in order to create a truly supportive learning environment, school counselors and teachers must work together.

How do we make school counseling a central part of the education system rather than an afterthought?

- By showing that counseling is not just for students in trouble, but for every student.

- By integrating social-emotional development into daily school life, just as we do with academic subjects.

- By advocating for the profession, educating staff and administrators on the value of counseling.

This book will explore key themes such as leadership, advocacy, social-emotional development, and the integration of counseling with instruction. These are the foundations of effective school counseling. When we understand our role, communicate our value, and work collaboratively with educators, we create schools where students are not only academically prepared but also emotionally strong and ready for the future.

The Growing Challenges in School Counseling

School counselors play a crucial role in student development, yet our profession is often overlooked. The education system prioritizes instruction—teaching students how to read, write, solve math problems, and think critically. While these skills are essential, academic success does not happen in isolation. Students also need emotional and social support to thrive, and that is where school counseling comes in.

One of the biggest struggles I faced as a school counselor was getting people to recognize the value of what we do. Teachers, administrators, and even parents often misunderstand school counseling. Many see counseling as something only for students who are "in trouble" or experiencing extreme difficulties. There is also a long-standing stigma around counseling in general, with many associating it with mental illness or dysfunction. But school counseling is not about diagnosing problems—it is about fostering development. It is about helping students build the emotional intelligence, coping skills, and resilience they need to succeed academically and in life.

Despite its importance, school counseling faces major obstacles, including:

- **Increased demand for mental health support** – Students today face more emotional challenges than ever, from anxiety and trauma to the effects of social media and economic hardship.

The need for school counseling has never been greater, especially after the pandemic. Many students are struggling with grief, isolation, and instability. The empowerment gap continues to grow, particularly in areas with high poverty, homelessness, and violence. Schools, however, tend to focus only on increasing academic instruction, without recognizing that students cannot learn effectively if their emotional needs are ignored.

Another emerging challenge is the rise in migrant and undocumented student populations. In cities like New York, many children come from families that fear deportation. Some students stop attending school altogether because their families are afraid. These are real issues that impact education, yet school counselors are often left to handle them alone, without the necessary support or resources.

I faced similar challenges. I had to research on my own, develop my own strategies, and find ways to advocate for students while also advocating for my profession.

The Lack of Professional Supervision and Support for School Counselors

One of the biggest challenges in school counseling is the lack of professional supervision. Teachers have assistant principals and principals who were once teachers themselves. These leaders are experts in instruction, capable of identifying teachers who may be going through a rough patch and providing hands-on support. They can observe lessons, offer feedback, and model best practices to help teachers improve.

However, school counselors do not have that same level of professional guidance. In many schools, especially at the elementary level, there is no supervisor with a counseling background who can provide professional support. If a counselor is struggling, there is no one to step in and say, "Here is the best way to conduct an individual session," or "This is how you should structure a small group counseling session." There is no one to guide them through best practices for classroom presentations or how to conduct an effective workshop. Instead, many counselors are left to figure things out on their own, without mentorship or structured professional development.

I experienced this firsthand. When I faced a hurdle of some sort, I had no one to turn to for advice. The principal expected me to know what to do simply because I had a degree in counseling. I was often told, *"Isn't this what you were trained for?"* But having a degree does not mean you stop learning once you enter the profession. Education and professional growth must continue. Best practices evolve, new challenges emerge, and ongoing training is essential. This is the message I emphasize to my graduate students: *earning your degree is just the beginning—you must continue to develop your skills throughout your career.*

The lack of structured supervision in school counseling contributes to the ongoing struggle for professional recognition. Many people still do not understand what school counselors do. They assume that if a student sees a counselor, it must mean something is "wrong" with them. There is a persistent belief that counseling is only for students with behavioral or mental health issues. But school counseling is not about diagnosing problems—it is about development. Our role is to ensure that every student gains the skills they need to succeed academically, socially, and emotionally.

This misunderstanding, combined with the lack of professional support, is one of the reasons I felt compelled to take action. Many educators recognize these issues, but I saw little being done to change them. I had hoped that after the pandemic, school districts would invest more in counseling services, but that has not been the case. Instead, we are seeing budget cuts, even as student needs grow.

Technology has also added new layers of emotional challenges that we are not fully addressing. When I was growing up, we did not have the internet, social media, or video games in the way students do today. We focused on real human interaction. But now, technology influences nearly every aspect of students' lives, sometimes in ways that negatively impact their emotional well-being. Yet, we are not providing the necessary support to help them navigate these challenges.

As a result, we are losing students academically. I see it even at the college level—many students today are less prepared than those from previous generations, despite having more access to technology and information. This is not just an academic issue; it is an emotional and social issue as well. If we do not invest in school counseling and recognize its role in student success, we will continue to see students struggle.

This book is my contribution to addressing these challenges. It is not enough to simply acknowledge the problems—we must take action to create real change. School counselors need proper supervision, ongoing professional development, and recognition as an essential part of the education system. Only then can we truly support students in both their academic and personal growth.

The Role of School Counseling in Personal Development

One of the biggest shortcomings of our education system is its lack of focus on personal development. When I look at other schooling systems, such as in Japan, I see a structured approach to building responsible, well-rounded individuals. In Japanese schools, students are given time to engage in social activities that teach them responsibility, teamwork, and communication. They take part in cleaning their classrooms, preparing meals, and sharing responsibilities with their peers. These activities shape them into active members of their community, giving them a sense of responsibility and a connection to the real world.

In contrast, when I was in school, we did not have dedicated time for such activities. There was no set period where we could talk to someone about personal challenges or seek guidance on how to handle social and emotional struggles. School counseling, in many cases, was either absent or undervalued. And from what I observe today, this gap still exists in many public schools.

This lack of focus on personal growth is one of the reasons why so many young people today struggle with identity, self-worth, and emotional instability. Without structured guidance, students may feel lost, disconnected, and unable to navigate the challenges of growing up. They may turn to unhealthy coping mechanisms, struggle with anxiety and depression, or even head down destructive paths.

When I began my career as a school counselor, I worked in private schools. In private schools, there was often a clearer expectation that counselors would support students beyond academics—helping them develop social skills, manage emotions, and prepare for the future. But in many public schools, this role was either overlooked or limited due to resource constraints. If schools truly prioritized personal development, we would see more students growing into confident, capable individuals.

The impact of this shift would be significant. We would not only see academic success improve, but we would also raise a generation of responsible citizens—future entrepreneurs, social workers, leaders, and changemakers. Instead of young people struggling with mental health challenges in isolation, they would have the tools to manage their emotions and build resilience. Instead of feeling disconnected from society, they would learn teamwork and leadership skills that would serve them throughout their lives.

Unfortunately, our public school system has never truly considered personal development as a priority. It has always been treated as an afterthought, rather than an essential part of education. But personal grooming—teaching students how to navigate life, relationships, and emotions—is just as important as academic knowledge. Schools must recognize that education is not just about producing test scores; it is about shaping individuals who can contribute meaningfully to society.

If we make personal development a priority, we will not only see fewer students struggling with anxiety and depression, but we will also foster a stronger, more responsible, and more capable generation. This is why school counseling is so important. It is not just about addressing problems—it is about preparing students for life.

The Stigma of Counseling and Its Role in Personal Growth

We live in a society where we interact with others every day. No one exists in isolation. No matter what profession a person chooses, social skills are necessary for success. Whether you are a doctor, teacher, engineer, or business owner, you must communicate, collaborate, and build relationships with others. However, one of the biggest challenges we face today is a decline in social skills, particularly among younger generations.

The pandemic played a major role in this issue. For a period of time, children and teenagers were isolated, unable to engage in normal social interactions. Remote learning replaced in-person education. Many students missed out on playing sports, attending school events, or even just having casual conversations with their peers. For some, even basic social experiences like going on a first date or hanging out with friends were put on hold.

Beyond the lack of socialization, there was also a great deal of fear and uncertainty. Many young people lived with the constant anxiety of whether their loved ones would survive. The stress of illness, financial struggles, and general instability created a lasting impact. And trauma is not something that disappears overnight. It lingers, often surfacing when we least expect it. Certain triggers—such as a difficult situation at school, rejection from a peer, or even a stressful work environment—can bring back those feelings of fear and insecurity.

Despite these challenges, our society still does not fully appreciate the value of counseling. In many cases, seeking counseling is viewed negatively. When someone says they are in counseling, others often assume there is something wrong with them. Instead of seeing counseling as a tool for growth, people associate it with weakness or dysfunction.

I have personally seen this stigma in schools. When I worked as Director of Student Support Services with high schools, many school counselors told me how difficult it was to get students to seek help. Adolescents, in particular, are highly concerned with how their peers perceive them. Many of them believe that going to a school counselor would make them seem 'different' or 'broken.' They fear being judged, so they avoid seeking the help they may desperately need.

But the truth is, counseling should not be viewed as something negative. It is not just for those who are struggling. It is for anyone who wants to grow, learn, and improve their life. Counseling provides guidance, helps individuals understand themselves better, and equips them with tools to navigate challenges.

We need to normalize counseling as part of healthy development. Instead of treating it as something only for those in crisis, we should recognize it as a valuable resource for anyone striving to reach their goals. Whether it is managing stress, improving relationships, or planning for the future, counseling can provide clarity and support.

Now, more than ever, we need to embrace counseling as a necessary part of education and life. The world is becoming increasingly complex, and young people need support to navigate the challenges ahead. If we shift our perspective and remove the stigma, we can create a society where seeking guidance is seen as a sign of strength, not weakness.

Chapter 1:
The History of Counsellng in the United States

To fully understand the role of school counselors today, it is imperative to look back at the history of school counseling in the United States. The profession began in the early 1900s as a response to the rapid changes brought about by industrialization, urban growth, and increased immigration. At that time, there was a strong need for vocational guidance to help young people prepare for work in a changing economy. School counseling was first introduced to support students in making career decisions and developing the skills needed to succeed in the workforce.

The early roots of school counseling can be traced to figures like Jesse B. Davis, who is often recognized as one of the pioneers of the field. He introduced vocational guidance programs into public schools in the early 20th century, helping students make informed choices about their futures. Around the same time, Frank Parsons, known as the "father of vocational guidance," emphasized the importance of matching a person's skills and interests with the needs of the labor market. His work laid the foundation for structured career counseling programs across schools in the United States.

As the educational system expanded, so did the responsibilities of school counselors. The role evolved from focusing solely on vocational guidance to addressing a broader range of student needs, including academic support, personal development, and social-emotional wellness. The changing landscape of education, as well as increasing awareness of student mental health, led to a more comprehensive view of what school counseling should offer.

Over time, different states began developing their own models for school counseling, which led to inconsistencies in the delivery of services and the expectations placed on school counselors. To address this, the American School Counselor Association (ASCA) introduced a national model. The ASCA National Model outlines a clear structure for effective school counseling programs. It focuses on academic development, career readiness, and social-emotional growth, providing a standard framework that schools across the country can follow.

However, many State models differ from the ASCA National Model. These differences can create confusion and gaps in implementation. Some states provide clear guidance and support for school counselors, while others offer limited structure, leaving individual schools to define the counselor's role on their own. This inconsistency impacts how well school counseling programs serve students and whether counselors can fully perform their duties.

A 2025 peer-reviewed article titled *"School Counseling Roles Across States: A Content Analysis Using the ASCA National Model"* examined how well state-level school counseling policies align with the

ASCA National Model's four core components—Define, Manage, Deliver, and Assess. The study reviewed policies across all 50 U.S. states and Washington, D.C., and revealed significant variation in the extent to which state frameworks reflect the national standard.

While some states have developed comprehensive policies that align closely with the ASCA model and provide clear, structured guidance for school counselors, others offer limited or vague direction, leaving individual districts or schools to define counselor roles on their own. These inconsistencies often result in uneven implementation of school counseling programs and can impact the overall quality of services provided to students. (Frank et al., 2025)

The study underscores that while the ASCA National Model offers a robust foundation, the effectiveness of school counseling across the country is largely dependent on local and state-level support, policy development, and resource allocation. This reinforces the need to examine national and state-level models side by side to identify opportunities for alignment and advocate for stronger, more consistent frameworks that support the profession.

Comparing and contrasting the national model with state-level models allows us to see where alignment exists and where improvements are needed. While the ASCA National Model provides a solid foundation, the success of school counseling programs often depends on local policies, resources, and the support provided at the district and school levels.

Understanding the evolution of school counseling and the differences between national and state approaches is key to strengthening the profession. It also helps us advocate for stronger policies, better training, and greater recognition of the important work that school counselors do every day.

The Impact of Industrialization and Economic Shifts on the Development of School Counseling

The rise of industrialization in the late 19th and early 20th centuries led to major changes in the American economy. Following the swift expansion of factories, businesses, and urban centers, a strong demand emerged for workers who could perform specific tasks in an organized and efficient way. This shift created a new hurdle for schools to overcome, which were now expected to prepare students not only academically but also for future careers in an industrial society.

As the country transitioned from an agricultural economy to an industrial one, schools began to emphasize the importance of career readiness. This resulted in the development of vocational guidance programs, which were designed to help students identify their interests, understand their strengths, and find suitable career paths. Educators and policymakers recognized that students needed more than just academic instruction—they also needed direction and support in planning their futures.

The early development of school counseling in the United States was heavily influenced by the rapid industrialization and economic transformation of the early 20th century. During this time, the rise of factories and urban employment opportunities created a growing need for vocational guidance in schools. The focus shifted from purely academic instruction to helping students understand their strengths and interests concerning the job market.

Influential figures like Jesse B. Davis and Frank Parsons were instrumental in formalizing this process—Davis by integrating career guidance into English classes, and Parsons by founding the Vocation Bureau in Boston in 1908, which emphasized aligning personal aptitude with career choice. These developments marked the beginning of school counseling as a means of supporting students' transition into the workforce, showing that the profession emerged not just to support student development but also to respond to broader economic demands (PsyWellPath, n.d).

School counseling became a way to bridge the gap between education and the workforce. Counselors were introduced into schools to guide students in making choices that aligned with both their personal goals and the demands of the job market. The focus on career readiness influenced the identity of the school counselor as someone who not only student development but also on economic progress by preparing young people to enter the workforce successfully.

This early foundation set the stage for a more comprehensive approach to counseling, one that would later expand to include academic, personal, and social-emotional development. However, the emphasis on career readiness remains a core part of school counseling today, especially as economic fluctuations continue to influence the expectations placed on students and educators.

The Influence of Major Educational Reforms and the Role of Professional Associations

The development of school counseling in the United States has been significantly shaped by federal educational policies and national reforms. Legislative actions such as the *Elementary and Secondary Education Act (ESEA)* of 1965 and the *No Child Left Behind Act (NCLB)* of 2001 initiated structural shifts in the way schools operated, and in turn, redefined the role and priorities of school counselors. These reforms highlighted the growing need for accountability in education, placing pressure on schools to produce measurable academic outcomes. As a result, school counselors were increasingly called upon to support not only the academic success of students but also their personal development and college and career pathways.

The ESEA laid the foundation for federal involvement in public education, targeting funding to schools in low-income areas and promoting equal access to education. Although counseling was not initially the focus, the act created a platform where support services could be included in discussions around student achievement. Later amendments to ESEA and programs such as Title I funding began to recognize counseling as a valuable support for students facing social and academic barriers.

With the passage of NCLB, accountability became even more central. Schools were required to meet specific performance benchmarks, and counselors were often expected to assist in identifying at-risk students, reducing dropout rates, and ensuring that students were prepared for standardized testing. This shifted the counselor's role from a traditional focus on vocational guidance to a broader, more complex set of responsibilities tied to school-wide outcomes.

According to Dahir and Stone (2009), school counselors have increasingly aligned their programs with accountability mandates set forth by federal policies such as ESEA and NCLB. The authors describe how counselors adopted action-research methods—specifically the MEASURE model—which allowed them to use data in conjunction with school improvement proactively note that accountability is now woven into the daily practices of counseling, replacing outdated "bean-counting" approaches with structured efforts to monitor data on attendance, grades, and discipline, collaboratively work with administrators and teachers, and implement targeted interventions.

This data-driven approach not only fosters school improvement but also positions counselors as key change agents in advancing student achievement and systemic equity (Dahir & Stone, 2009).

At the same time, the establishment and growth of the *American School Counselor Association (ASCA)* played a critical role in the professionalization of school counseling. ASCA provided a national model to define the scope, competencies, and ethical standards of the profession. The *ASCA National Model* emphasized a comprehensive approach, integrating academic, career, and social-emotional development into a unified framework. This model also promoted the importance of statistics-driven practices, collaboration with educators and families, and advocacy for equitable student outcomes.

While the ASCA National Model offers consistency, each state interprets and implements school counseling practices differently. State-specific models vary in terms of counselor-to-student ratios, allocated counseling time, and defined roles. Comparing these models helps highlight the need for more standardized approaches that still account for regional needs and school-level realities.

The Gradual Expansion of School Counseling and the Impact of Societal Change

The scope of school counseling in the United States has expanded significantly since its early focus on vocational guidance. In its initial form, counseling was primarily concerned with helping students make career decisions and prepare for employment after high school. However, as the social landscape of the country changed, so did the responsibilities of school counselors. This shift was not sudden but rather the result of evolving needs within the student population and growing recognition of the importance of mental and emotional well-being.

Beginning in the mid-20th century, school counselors began to play a more active role in addressing students' personal and social concerns. Factors such as family stress, peer relationships, and emotional development began to emerge as critical components of student success. As these needs became more visible in school settings, counselors adapted their practice to offer more comprehensive support.

The Civil Rights Movement was a significant turning point. As schools became more diverse, counselors were called upon to support students from a wide range of racial, cultural, and economic backgrounds. The rising demand for equity in education highlighted the importance of culturally responsive counseling and advocacy for underrepresented student groups. Counselors were increasingly expected to serve as advocates for social justice within schools, ensuring that all students had access to the resources and support necessary for success.

At the same time, awareness of mental health issues began to grow in the broader society. Psychological research and public discourse emphasized the long-term impact of untreated mental health problems, especially in children and adolescents. Schools, as central institutions in students' lives, became key sites for early identification and intervention. This required school counselors to acquire additional training and skills, including those related to mental health screening, crisis response, and coordination with outside mental health providers.

A comprehensive historical overview notes that in the 1960s, spurred by the Civil Rights Movement and shifting societal needs, U.S. school systems expanded their focus beyond vocational planning to addressing students' social and emotional health.

During this period, the *Community Mental Health Act of 1963* provided federal funding for community mental health centers and expanded the school's role to support the integration of mental wellness in education. This federal initiative catalyzed the development of graduate-level counseling programs and formal licensure requirements, solidifying the school counselor's role as part of the educational team.

Furthermore, historical analysis traces how schools became primary sites for mental health intervention, requiring counselors to incorporate techniques such as mental health screening, crisis management, and collaboration with external providers. These enhancements in counselor training and professional standards reflected a broader trend toward recognizing and responding to students' psychological needs.

Together, these developments—rooted in Civil Rights–era reforms and public health policy—transformed the school counseling profession, embedding mental health competencies, standardized education, and formal qualifications into its foundation. (Walker, 2018)

These societal changes helped elevate the profession and led to the further development of standards and training requirements. The establishment of graduate-level counseling programs, licensure requirements, and professional associations formalized the role of the school counselor as an essential part of the educational team.

Organizations such as the American School Counselor Association (ASCA) began to redefine the profession by promoting a more holistic model of student support. The ASCA National Model encouraged school counselors to work across three domains—academic, career, and social-emotional development—while also promoting leadership, advocacy, collaboration, and systemic change. This shift placed counselors at the center of efforts to improve school climate, reduce disparities, and support the whole child.

Despite national guidelines, many states adopted their own models for school counseling, reflecting differences in funding, staffing, and local priorities. These models vary widely in how they define counselor roles, expected outcomes, and time allocation. Comparing and contrasting these state-level models with the ASCA National Model is essential in understanding the inconsistent implementation of school counseling services across the country and the need for a more unified approach that still respects local context.

The Role of Professional Organizations and the Emergence of State Models

Professional organizations have played a key role in the development and recognition of school counseling as a distinct and vital profession within the American educational system. Among these, the American School Counselor Association (ASCA) has had the most significant influence. Since its founding in 1952, ASCA has worked to establish national standards for the training, practice, and evaluation of school counselors. These efforts have helped unify the field, elevate its status, and clarify the expectations placed on school counselors in both academic and non-academic areas.

One of ASCA's most important contributions has been the development of the ASCA National Model. This framework outlines a comprehensive, data-driven approach to school counseling, designed to support students in three primary domains: academic development, career readiness, and social-emotional growth. The model emphasizes the use of data to assess needs and measure impact, and it encourages school counselors to take on leadership roles within their schools. It also defines clear goals and activities, advocating for school counseling programs that are proactive, equitable, and focused on promoting systemic change.

A 2012 study by Palmer and Erford utilized the ASCA Program Audit to assess how the level of implementation of the ASCA National Model correlates with student outcomes in suburban Maryland school districts.

The audit measured program implementation across over 100 schools at the elementary, middle, and high school levels. The results revealed that higher implementation of the ASCA model significantly predicted improved outcomes in high school, including better performance in English and algebra, higher attendance rates, and a trend toward increased graduation rates. While correlations at the elementary and middle school levels were weaker, the study highlights that fully implemented, data-driven counseling programs aligned with the ASCA model can have a meaningful impact on student achievement and engagement at the high school level, reinforcing the value of comprehensive, structured counseling frameworks (Palmer & Erford, 2012).

The ASCA National Model has helped to standardize school counseling across the United States, offering a consistent foundation for counselor preparation programs, professional development, and district-level evaluation. However, education policy and school funding remain primarily under the control of individual states. As a result, many states have developed their own models for school counseling, which may align with the ASCA framework to varying degrees.

These state-specific models often reflect local educational priorities, budget constraints, and cultural considerations. Some states have adopted the ASCA model nearly in full, integrating it into their counselor evaluation tools, certification standards, and school accountability systems. Others have developed independent models that define counselor roles more narrowly, often placing a stronger emphasis on academic advising or college and career readiness. In certain cases, school counselors are still viewed primarily as administrative staff, responsible for scheduling or discipline-related tasks, rather than as mental health professionals or student advocates.

The differences between state models and the ASCA framework can create confusion about the purpose and potential of school counseling. This inconsistency has led to varied levels of support, staffing, and recognition for school counselors across the country. While some districts provide structured counseling programs supported by leadership and supervision, others continue to treat counseling as a secondary or optional service. These discrepancies can impact student outcomes, especially in underserved communities where school counselors may be the only accessible mental health professionals.

To strengthen the profession, it is important to continue advocating for greater alignment between state models and the ASCA National Model. Doing so ensures that all students, regardless of where they live, have access to comprehensive and high-quality counseling services. Additionally, increased collaboration between state departments of education and national organizations can help improve counselor preparation, promote best practices, and address long-standing challenges such as staffing shortages and a lack of professional support.

Defining the Role of the School Counselor Within the Educational System

One of the most persistent challenges facing school counselors is the ongoing struggle to clearly define their role within the broader educational system. Although professional organizations such as the American School Counselor Association (ASCA) have worked to create national standards, there is still significant variation in how school counselors are viewed and utilized in different schools and districts. This lack of consistency has often led to confusion among instructional staff, administrators, and even school counselors themselves.

School counselors are trained to provide academic, social-emotional, and career support to students, yet their roles are frequently misunderstood or minimized. In some schools, counselors are asked to take on administrative tasks such as scheduling, lunch duty, standardized test coordination, or attendance tracking—duties that do not align with the professional training or primary function of a counselor. These responsibilities can take time away from direct student services and limit the counselor's ability to address students' developmental needs in a meaningful and proactive way.

This role confusion is further complicated by the pressure school administrators face to meet academic benchmarks and compliance requirements. In environments where test scores and graduation rates are prioritized above all else, the value of school counseling may be overlooked or reduced to basic academic advising. As a result, many counselors find themselves in positions where they are expected to support instructional goals without being seen as essential contributors to student development.

Efforts to clarify the counselor's role must begin with a shared understanding between administrators, teachers, and counseling staff about the unique contributions that school counselors make. When counselors are recognized as key partners in the educational process—professionals who work to remove barriers to learning and support the whole child—schools are better positioned to foster student success. Establishing clearly defined job descriptions, providing professional development, and aligning with national and state models can help ensure that school counselors are used effectively and remain focused on what they do best: supporting student growth and achievement.

A doctoral study conducted in 2022 examined how intentional collaboration between a school counselor and a high school administrator influenced clarity of role expectations and student support outcomes. Through monthly structured meetings and the use of tools recommended by ASCA—such as the Administrator Conference Template (ACT)—the pair established clear, shared goals focused on improving postsecondary planning.

Over the school year, their alignment grew significantly: what began with misaligned perceptions of duties evolved into a trusting and goal-oriented partnership. This collaboration led to improved communication, intentional use of counselor time, and data-driven decisions to address student needs. The structured check-ins helped build continuity and allowed both professionals to monitor progress, tackle obstacles, and adjust strategies dynamically. Their work resulted in stronger shared accountability, reduced role ambiguity, and a more coherent focus on supporting student growth, illustrating how clearly defined roles, ongoing dialogue, and alignment with ASCA tools can enhance student-centered practice and underscore the counselor's role as a key educational partner (Doe, 2024).

Milestones in the Advancement of School Counseling: Graduate Programs and Data-Driven Practice

The development of school counseling as a profession is marked by several key milestones that have helped define and elevate its role in education. Among the most significant of these milestones is the establishment of formal graduate programs specifically designed to train school counselors. These programs emerged in response to the growing recognition that counselors require specialized knowledge and skills to address the complex academic, emotional, and social needs of students. Prior to the creation of these programs, many individuals entered the profession with general teaching credentials or limited training in counseling theory and practice.

Graduate programs began to include comprehensive coursework in developmental psychology, counseling ethics, multicultural competency, group counseling, and career development. This structured preparation laid the foundation for a more professional and accountable field, allowing school counselors to apply research-based strategies in real-time school environments. Accreditation by organizations such as the Council for Accreditation of Counseling and Related Educational Programs (CACREP) has since become an important standard for ensuring the quality and consistency of counselor education programs across institutions.

Another major shift in the field has been the integration of data-driven counseling strategies. As educational accountability increased in the late 20th and early 21st centuries, schools were called to demonstrate measurable results in both academic performance and student well-being. School counselors responded to this shift by incorporating data collection and analysis into their practice. This included the use of student achievement data, attendance records, behavioral referrals, and needs assessments to identify trends, set goals, and evaluate the impact of counseling interventions.

A 2022 brief led by researchers from Harvard University underscores the transformative impact of data-driven strategies in school counseling. The report explains that high-quality counseling programs are "preventative and use data to target student needs better," integrating academic, social-emotional, and postsecondary development goals.

It emphasizes that counselors who leverage student performance data, attendance records, behavioral incidents, and survey feedback can more precisely identify at-risk students, develop targeted interventions, and assess program effectiveness. Additionally, the brief highlights that lowering student-to-counselor ratios enhances the capacity for meaningful data use and relationship-building.

This aligns with your points: as educational accountability increased, counselors began systematically collecting and analyzing multiple data sources—such as achievement, attendance, behavioral referrals, and needs assessments—to set goals and evaluate the impact of their interventions. Through these evidence-based, outcome-driven approaches, school counselors have demonstrated the effectiveness of their work and strengthened their role as key contributors to schoolwide improvement efforts (Savitz-Romer & Nicola, 2022).

The emphasis on data has helped school counselors demonstrate the effectiveness of their work and advocate for appropriate roles within their schools. Through the use of evidence-based programs and outcome measurements, counselors are able to justify their contributions and align their work with school-wide improvement efforts. These advancements have strengthened the profession and positioned school counselors as essential members of the educational team, particularly when guided by national frameworks such as the ASCA National Model.

The history of school counseling is not only a record of how the profession has developed but also a guide for how it continues to respond to present-day demands. Understanding the milestones and changes from the early days of vocational guidance to the introduction of mental health and academic support provides valuable context for the modern school counselor's role. These historical foundations have helped shape a profession that now addresses supporting academic achievement, career development, and social-emotional well-being.

The evolution of school counseling practices has often been influenced by broader societal and educational changes. For instance, the Civil Rights Movement pushed counselors to consider issues of equity and access, which remain central to the profession today. The rise of mental health awareness and the growing number of students facing complex life challenges have further expanded the counselor's responsibilities. These shifts have required school counselors to build a more comprehensive skill set and to adopt practices grounded in research, ethics, and cultural responsiveness.

In today's environment, school counselors are expected to do more with fewer resources. Challenges such as high student-to-counselor ratios, unclear job expectations, and limited access to supervision or professional development create barriers to effectiveness. Despite these obstacles, the profession continues to adapt. The American School Counselor Association (ASCA) National Model serves as a guiding framework, offering structure and clarity for the implementation of best practices. Many states have developed their own models, which may align with or diverge from the national approach, reflecting the unique needs and policies of local communities.

Modern school counseling is rooted in the belief that data-informed decision-making and student-centered planning can drive meaningful outcomes. By looking to the past, counselors can recognize how far the field has come and how it must continue to evolve. Reflecting on these developments helps today's school counselors remain grounded in foundational values while staying flexible and innovative in the face of changing student needs and educational expectations.

$$\smile\!\!\!\curvearrowright$$

Chapter 2:
Rationale for School Counseling

The primary purpose of school counseling extends far beyond assisting students with academic concerns. At its core, school counseling is designed to foster overall student development by addressing not only academic needs but also social, emotional, and behavioral growth. This comprehensive approach reflects a deep understanding that student success is not confined to test scores or classroom performance, but rather, is predicated upon a broad set of life experiences, internal resources, and environmental factors.

Over the years, the field of education has gradually embraced a more holistic framework, one that recognizes the interconnected nature of learning, behavior, and emotional well-being. School counselors play a significant role in this framework. By focusing on the whole child, they help create supportive educational environments where students can thrive both inside and outside the classroom. The American School Counselor Association (ASCA) has been instrumental in defining this role through its national model, which outlines the academic, career, and social-emotional domains of student development. State-specific models have often adopted similar frameworks, though there are differences in implementation and emphasis that reflect local needs and policy priorities.

In the International Journal of Environmental Research and Public Health, a 2022 article highlights the critical role schools play in advancing students' well-being throughout their development. It emphasizes that adopting a holistic, whole-school approach is essential, one that supports academic, physical, cognitive, social, and emotional growth. By building a positive environment rooted in secure relationships and attention to student wellness, schools can mitigate the effects of trauma and foster long-term resilience. This approach has been shown to boost academic achievement, behavior, social skills, student engagement, and overall satisfaction while simultaneously reducing suspensions and disciplinary incidents (Gordillo & Haring, 2025).

Today's students face increasing challenges that can interfere with learning. Rates of anxiety, depression, family instability, and community violence are steadily rising. Many students find it hard to manage these pressures, and their ability to concentrate, form relationships, and make responsible decisions is often compromised. In this climate, school counselors are not merely helpful; they have proved to be essential. Their training enables them to identify early signs of distress, provide direct support, and refer students to appropriate outside services when necessary. They are also equipped to deliver preventive programs and interventions that promote resilience, empathy, and conflict resolution.

As educational systems evolve, the need for school counselors who are trained to address diverse student needs continues to grow. Effective counseling programs contribute not only to academic success but also to improved student behavior, school climate, and family engagement. By maintaining strong partnerships with teachers, parents, and administrators, counselors ensure that support for students is coordinated and continuous. In this way, school counseling has become an indispensable element of modern education, an essential service that reinforces the mission of schools to develop capable, confident, and well-rounded individuals prepared for future challenges.

Redefining the Role of School Counselors: From Crisis Responders to Developmental Leaders

A common misconception surrounding school counseling is that it is primarily a reactive service, only necessary when students face crises. While crisis intervention remains an important function, this limited view does not reflect the entire scope of the profession. School counselors are trained to deliver preventive and developmental services that are critical for student growth over time. By offering structured programs that address emotional regulation, study habits, social skills, and career awareness, counselors help students build the tools needed to succeed both academically and personally.

The American School Counselor Association (ASCA) national model supports a proactive approach by emphasizing the delivery of services through a comprehensive counseling program. This model encourages school counselors to work with all students, not just those in immediate distress. Many state models mirror this framework, though implementation often varies based on funding, staffing, and local policy. In schools where the role of the counselor is well integrated into the educational mission, students benefit from early support and consistent guidance. This reduces the need for emergency interventions and promotes a culture of continuous development.

Research consistently shows that there is a strong link between student well-being and academic performance. Students who feel safe, supported, and emotionally stable are more likely to attend school regularly, engage in class, and perform better on assessments. Emotional difficulties, when left unaddressed, can disrupt concentration, lower motivation, and result in behavioral challenges. School counselors play a central role in identifying these issues early and implementing strategies to reduce their impact on learning.

A contemporary meta-analysis published in Child Development (Cipriano et al., 2023) reviewed 424 universal school-based SEL programs across 53 countries, involving over 575,000 students. The findings indicate that, compared to control groups, participants in SEL interventions demonstrated significant improvements in social-emotional skills, peer relationships, school functioning, school climate and safety, and academic achievement. These results underscore the transformative potential of SEL programs in fostering holistic student development and strengthening school environments.

In this context, school counselors become a bridge between emotional health and academic success. Their work helps to create environments where students are prepared to learn and grow. School systems must recognize the value of proactive counseling and invest in models that allow counselors to focus on prevention as well as intervention. By doing so, schools can move away from outdated views of counseling as a reactive service and instead see it as a vital part of the educational process.

School Counseling and Early Intervention

The field of school counseling has increasingly embraced data-driven strategies and evidence-based interventions to demonstrate its effectiveness in improving student outcomes. This shift supports not only more precise planning and delivery of services but also allows school leaders and policymakers to better understand the measurable value of comprehensive school counseling programs. By using data to guide practice, school counselors are better positioned to advocate for their role and secure necessary support and resources.

A 2019 report from the American School Counselor Association (ASCA) highlights that schools implementing comprehensive, data-informed counseling programs consistently show improvements in key areas such as student attendance, academic achievement, and behavior management. These outcomes are especially evident in schools that fully adhere to the ASCA National Model. One widely cited study published in *Professional School Counseling* found that students attending schools with fully implemented ASCA-aligned programs reported feeling safer and more connected to their school environment. They also showed improved academic performance on standardized tests, which supports the argument that school counseling contributes directly to student success (Lapan, Gysbers, & Kayson, 2007).

School counselors use tools such as needs assessments, student surveys, behavior incident tracking, and academic performance monitoring to identify patterns and intervene early. These tools help determine which students are at risk and allow for targeted support before problems escalate. Early intervention is particularly critical at the elementary level, where foundational skills in emotional regulation, problem-solving, and social interaction are still forming.

Addressing these areas early contributes to long-term academic and personal development.

The ASCA National Model emphasizes the importance of using outcome data to evaluate the effectiveness of counseling activities and make informed adjustments. Although many states have developed their own counseling frameworks inspired by the national model, the degree of implementation varies widely. Some state models lack the structure, accountability, or funding necessary to replicate the successes documented under ASCA guidelines. Comparing the national framework to state-specific models can reveal discrepancies in practice and help identify areas where additional training, resources, or policy alignment may be needed.

Early Intervention in Elementary School

The importance of early intervention in school counseling cannot be overstated. The elementary school years serve as a critical period in a child's development, where foundational emotional, behavioral, and social skills are established. These formative years significantly influence future academic success, personal well-being, and the ability to form healthy relationships. Intervening early allows school counselors to provide the tools and support students need to navigate their educational journey with resilience and confidence.

A growing body of research supports the positive impact of early social and emotional learning (SEL) initiatives. A comprehensive meta-analysis conducted by Durlak et al. (2011), which examined the outcomes of over 270,000 students across multiple school-based SEL programs, found that participation in such programs was associated with an average 11-percentile point gain in academic performance. These SEL efforts commonly include components led or supported by school counselors, focusing on emotional regulation, goal setting, empathy development, and conflict resolution.

When school counselors engage with students early in their academic careers, they are able to address challenges before they develop into more serious problems. For example, teaching students how to manage peer conflict or cope with anxiety during elementary school can prevent disciplinary issues, improve classroom engagement, and support stronger peer relationships. Additionally, early interventions reduce the need for reactive or crisis-based support in later grades. This proactive approach enhances school climate and increases the sense of safety and belonging among students. Modeling is a powerful teaching tool. Adults can influence student behavior by consistently demonstrating positive actions both inside and outside the classroom. Learning takes place in many forms, and the lessons gained through personal experiences often stay with us for a lifetime.

Counselors use a variety of tools to identify needs early, including behavioral observations, needs assessments, and collaboration with teachers and parents. These tools, aligned with the ASCA National Model, allow for data-informed decision-making and individualized support. The earlier counselors can identify and respond to concerns, the more effective their interventions become, leading to more consistent academic and behavioral outcomes. Early identification gives school counselors a chance to work closely with other school staff to solve problems using practical, solution-focused strategies. Taking the lead in collecting and analyzing data helps everyone at the school better understand student development and make informed decisions that support student success.

A 2023 survey of 500 U.S. K-12 school counselors conducted by Catapult Learning (in partnership with the National Center for

School Mental Health) found overwhelming agreement (94%) that proactive, early intervention strategies—rather than reactive crisis response—are crucial to preventing student mental health issues from escalating to Tier 3 crisis levels. Nearly all counselors (96%) believed that too many students were being pushed into crisis-level support unnecessarily and could benefit from earlier, preventive measures.

However, they reported feeling constrained by limited time and resources, with 63% noting they could not deliver adequate Tier 2 support. This gap not only undermines early intervention efforts but also impacts counselor well-being, with 90% stating that student mental health concerns significantly affect their own stress and work-life balance (Catapult Learning, 2025).

Ultimately, early intervention reinforces the idea that school counseling is not merely a supportive service but a vital component of student development. By addressing emotional and social challenges at a young age, counselors help create a strong foundation for lifelong learning and success. Schools that prioritize early counseling support are better positioned to foster well-rounded, resilient, and academically capable students.

School Counselors and Equity in a Digital Era

School counselors play a critical role in helping to close the opportunity gaps faced by students from diverse socioeconomic backgrounds, especially those in urban and underfunded school districts. These students often face a combination of academic, social, and emotional challenges that can affect their ability to succeed. School counselors provide consistent support by identifying barriers, advocating for student needs, and connecting families with academic and community resources that may otherwise be out of reach.

In low-income areas, students may lack access to quality healthcare, after-school programs, or stable home environments. Counselors in these settings often serve as the main link between students and the support systems necessary for their development. The ASCA National Model emphasizes equity and access as key components of effective counseling programs. It guides counselors to use data and targeted interventions to ensure every student is provided with the tools needed to achieve academic and personal excellence. Many state models adopt these principles, but there are differences in funding, training, and implementation. States with lower counselor-to-student ratios and fewer resources may struggle to deliver the same level of impact, even if the framework is in place.

There exists a significant disparity in counselor availability across states. Underfunded districts, often serving high numbers of low-income students and students of color, frequently have far higher student-to-counselor ratios than recommended levels. These imbalances hinder counselors' ability to provide equitable support for vulnerable students. The authors argue that such disparities raise serious ethical concerns and call for policy reforms and targeted investment to ensure counselors can deliver meaningful access and advocacy (Brown & Knight, 2024).

The role of counselors has also expanded due to the rise of digital distractions, social media use, and increasing dependency on technology. Students today face new challenges that affect their concentration, sleep patterns, and emotional well-being. Research from Common Sense Media (2023) shows that teens spend an average of over 8 hours per day on screens, often replacing in-person interactions and contributing to higher levels of anxiety and depression. Technology can support learning, but it cannot replace the value of real human interaction. Personal connections remain essential for emotional, social, and academic growth.

School counselors are often the first to observe these effects in the classroom. They work with teachers and parents to monitor behavior, teach digital literacy, and help students set healthy boundaries with technology. Programs aligned with the ASCA model include digital wellness education as part of a broader counseling curriculum. Some state models have begun incorporating similar content, but again, the level of detail and support can differ significantly. The responsible consumption of technology is an important skill for future success. It helps students make smart choices, stay safe, and use digital tools in positive and productive ways.

In both addressing equity and digital stressors, school counselors act as key advocates for the whole child. Their work supports a school culture that recognizes the needs of all students and responds to the demands of a changing social and technological environment.

School Counselors as Connectors and Long-Term Support Providers

School counselors hold a unique position within the educational system, serving as a vital bridge between students, teachers, parents, and administrators. Their role goes beyond academic planning or crisis response. Counselors are trained to listen, assess, and guide all members of the school community toward shared goals. Through their communication and collaboration skills, they help align student needs with available resources, ensure consistent support, and encourage a shared understanding of student development across all stakeholders.

A 2023 report from the RAMP (Recognized ASCA Model Program) initiative found that counselors in aligned schools engaged in weekly communication with teachers and administrators and regular meetings with parents, promoting equitable services, stronger student belonging, and enhanced recognition of the counseling program's impact. These findings affirm the counselor's authentic role as a liaison and systems collaborator who aligns student needs with school resources, fosters mutual understanding among stakeholders, and supports school-wide goals, consistent with both national standards and local practice (American School Counselor Association, 2023).

The American School Counselor Association (ASCA) National Model promotes a comprehensive approach that includes academic, career, and social-emotional development. It encourages school counselors to maintain clear communication with teachers to monitor student progress, coordinate with parents to offer insight into behavioral or emotional needs, and engage with administrators to advocate for systemic improvements. In many states, the local counseling models reflect these practices but may vary in how closely they follow ASCA's structured recommendations. Some state models offer broad guidance without the clear accountability measures or student outcome tracking promoted by the national model.

In this collaborative role, school counselors also influence the long-term development of students. Their work fosters early skills that are critical for future success, including emotional regulation, problem-solving, and decision-making. These skills not only help students cope with immediate challenges but also prepare them for post-secondary transitions. Counselors provide career exploration tools, college application support, and guidance on financial aid, helping students from all backgrounds see viable paths forward after graduation.

Studies have shown that students who participate in structured school counseling programs are more likely to feel connected to school and demonstrate better academic and social outcomes (Lapan, Gysbers, & Petroski, 2001). They are also more likely to report confidence in handling peer pressure, managing time, and setting personal goals. These are essential life skills that remain valuable well beyond the classroom.

Schools are part of a larger system that can be difficult to understand. Parents and students may often feel overwhelmed and may not have the information they need to succeed. School counselors are specially trained to help guide families through this system, giving them the support and knowledge needed to reach their goals.

The impact of a cohesive, well-supported school counseling program is long-lasting. When schools adopt the ASCA model and invest in trained, data-informed counselors, the results are visible in student achievement, reduced behavioral issues, and stronger school climates. Where state models mirror this national framework, outcomes tend to align more closely with the broader mission of whole-child development.

Recognizing Counseling as an Essential Service and the Value of Trauma-Informed Support

School counseling must be seen as a central and essential component of the educational system rather than as an optional or supportive service. As the needs of students continue to grow more complex, especially in areas of emotional health, trauma, and mental well-being, it is no longer acceptable to treat counseling as a secondary function within schools. School counselors are trained professionals who provide necessary guidance, and their work contributes directly to the academic, social, and emotional development of students. Without their involvement, many of the systemic challenges students face remain unaddressed.

The ASCA National Model clearly positions school counseling as a core element of student support. It outlines structured roles, encourages data-based decision making, and stresses the value of equitable access to counseling services for all students. The model also promotes advocacy as a key responsibility of school counselors, urging them to speak on behalf of students' needs and to work toward removing barriers that limit student potential. In contrast, some state models still define school counselors in limited ways, often focusing only on academic advising or test coordination. These narrower definitions restrict the counselor's ability to support students comprehensively and result in underfunded, understaffed counseling departments.

One of the most urgent areas in which school counselors are needed is trauma-informed care. Many students come to school with experiences of abuse, neglect, loss, or exposure to violence, and these adverse experiences have direct effects on behavior, concentration, and emotional regulation. Trauma-informed counseling practices recognize how these experiences affect learning and behavior and focus on building safe, trusting environments where students feel seen, heard, and respected. Counselors trained in trauma-informed care use strategies that reduce re-traumatization and foster resilience.

Trauma-informed approaches are not only beneficial to students with known trauma histories but also help create a supportive environment for all students. These practices include predictable routines, clear expectations, emotional check-ins, and consistent communication between school staff and families. Counselors also provide referrals to outside services and help connect families with community resources when needed. The ASCA National Model supports trauma-informed practices by encouraging collaboration with mental health providers, building partnerships with families, and promoting interventions that consider the whole child.

A recent research article published in Professional School Counseling provides specific guidance on how school counselors can deliver a trauma-informed care approach using a Multi-Tiered System of Supports (MTSS) framework to support youth in foster care. The study underscores that school counselors, serving as advocates, supporters, and change agents at various MTSS tiers, are vital to meeting the mental health needs of these vulnerable students.

By building trauma-sensitive comprehensive programs, counselors help foster safe and supportive school environments that promote learning and emotional well-being for all students, particularly for those affected by trauma. This evidence reinforces the essential role of counselors in integrating trauma awareness across prevention levels. It underscores the importance of training counselors in trauma-informed strategies to enhance student engagement and academic access (Martinez et al., 2019).

Despite the evidence supporting the role of school counselors and the benefits of trauma-informed programs, many school districts still allocate limited funding for counseling positions. Some schools employ only one counselor for hundreds of students, making it difficult to provide individualized support or proactive programming. The lack of funding, training, and staffing undermines the effectiveness of school counseling efforts and places additional burdens on teachers and administrators, who are not always equipped to address emotional and behavioral concerns.

In conclusion, it is essential for school systems to view counseling as a non-negotiable part of education. Following the ASCA National Model can guide districts in designing programs that reflect current student needs and encourage long-term success. When compared to more limited state models, the national framework offers clearer expectations and stronger accountability measures. Investing in well-trained, well-supported counselors who can deliver trauma-informed care is not only a moral obligation but also a practical step toward building healthier schools and communities.

∽◦

Chapter 3:
Different Levels of School Counseling and How They Operate

The role of the school counselor changes significantly as students transition through elementary, middle, and high school. Each stage presents distinct developmental, academic, and social-emotional needs that require tailored strategies and services. While the foundational principles of comprehensive school counseling remain consistent, the delivery of those services evolves in response to students' age, maturity, and life circumstances.

At the elementary level, school counselors focus primarily on prevention and early intervention. This includes promoting basic emotional regulation, fostering positive peer relationships, and facilitating the development of conflict resolution skills. Counselors often work in classrooms to deliver developmentally appropriate presentations on empathy, cooperation, and problem-solving. At this stage, students are forming their self-concept and learning how to navigate the school environment. The American School Counselor Association (ASCA) National Model encourages structured school counseling programs that help build these foundational skills. Many state models reflect similar priorities, although the availability of full-time counselors in elementary schools remains inconsistent across districts – partly because school counselors are not required except for students mandated to receive counseling.

Recent research underscores the importance of elementary school counselors' focus on prevention and early intervention through developmentally appropriate programming. A 2023 randomized controlled trial found that elementary students participating in a school-based social and emotional learning (SEL) intervention demonstrated significant gains in empathy, perspective-taking, and peer acceptance, reinforcing the value of early counseling in promoting positive peer relationships and social-emotional growth (PMC, 2023).

Similarly, another study on classroom-based interventions showed that children exposed to structured emotional learning activities exhibited improved emotion knowledge, stronger emotional regulation skills, and reductions in internalizing behaviors (PMC, 2015). These findings align with the American School Counselor Association (ASCA) National Model's emphasis on structured, proactive counseling programs that help children build foundational skills for academic and personal success (Al-Jbouri et al., 2023).

In middle school, the counselor's role expands to address more complex social pressures and academic challenges. Students in this age group experience significant physical, cognitive, and emotional changes. School counselors must help students manage increased academic demands, shifting peer dynamics, and growing self-awareness. Responsive services, such as small group counseling and individual planning, are becoming more common. Career awareness activities may also begin, providing students with an introduction to future pathways and helping them understand how current behaviors relate to long-term goals. The ASCA model emphasizes the importance of aligning counseling services with students' developmental tasks, and state-level guidelines generally support this progression. However, disparities in staffing and training sometimes limit the consistent application of these standards.

A 2024 systematic review published in a leading journal examined various career interventions for middle school students. It found that theories like Social Cognitive Career Theory (SCCT) and Career Construction Theory (CCT) effectively guide structured, developmentally appropriate career planning programs. Particularly, the review emphasized that a counselor's support is the most critical factor influencing the success of these interventions, helping students build confidence, explore interests, and begin connecting their emerging identities to academic and career choices (Tucker, 2025).

By the time students reach high school, counselors shift their focus to post-secondary planning, personal responsibility, and independence. Academic advisement, career and college readiness, and social-emotional support become core priorities. Counselors advise students in developing a comprehensive understanding of course selections and how these choices connect to future college, career, or military pathways. They also provide guidance on standardized test preparation and post-secondary application processes.

A 2025 analysis highlighted the strategic role high school counselors play in supporting course selection and post-secondary planning. Counselors assist students in aligning their coursework with college and career aspirations, offering personalized guidance that enhances long-term readiness. By helping students craft coherent academic roadmaps and encouraging realistic, goal-aligned course sequences, counselors become vital partners in both academic and future planning (Wang and Wang, 2025).

They also provide counseling for stress management, relationship concerns, and transitional anxiety as students prepare for life beyond high school. The ASCA National Model supports the integration of these services into a broader school improvement plan, ensuring that all students are guided toward successful adult outcomes.

State models vary in how these responsibilities are structured, with some emphasizing college preparation more heavily, while others highlight workforce preparation or social-emotional development.

Overall, the role of the school counselor must remain responsive to students' developmental stages while also reflecting the standards set by national and state models. A well-structured counseling program that adapts to students' evolving needs is critical in ensuring their academic success, emotional growth, and making sure they are equipped for any setback life hurls their way. Continued professional development and adequate staffing are essential to making this possible at every level of schooling.

Guiding Academic Transitions Across Educational Levels

One of the most important responsibilities of school counselors is to assist students and families as they prepare for key academic transitions. These transitions often occur at the end of elementary, middle, and high school when students must decide about the next phase of their education. The role of the counselor during these periods is not only to provide information, but to offer structured support that matches the developmental needs of the student. The American School Counselor Association (ASCA) National Model provides a framework for this work, emphasizing academic planning as a core component of a comprehensive school counseling program. State-level models also include similar goals, though the strategies used may vary based on regional priorities and available resources. School counselors work closely with teachers and other support staff to make sure their goals are aligned and that students receive consistent support across all areas of learning and development.

At the elementary level, school counselors help students understand what it means to move to middle school. While academic selection may not be as complex at this stage, students and parents often face decisions about which public or magnet programs to apply to, particularly in districts that offer specialized middle school tracks. Counselors provide age-appropriate classroom presentations and individual planning sessions to help students think about their learning styles, interests, and goals. These conversations begin to lay the foundation for informed decision-making. In districts that follow the ASCA model closely, there is an emphasis on making these conversations inclusive, proactive, and aligned with the student's broader developmental progress. School counselors are most effective when they collaborate with teachers to align their classroom presentations with the subjects and skills students are learning in class.

As students enter middle school, the decisions they face become more multifaceted. In many states, students need to choose among various high school programs, including college preparatory tracks, vocational-technical schools, and specialized academies. School counselors aid students and families in navigating these options by facilitating information sessions, career exploration workshops, and individual advising. They often collaborate with high school staff to provide orientation programs, school visits, or shadowing experiences. These activities are supported by the ASCA model's emphasis on academic and career planning, and they are reflected in many state frameworks. However, differences in staffing ratios, training, and resource allocation mean that access to these services is not always equitable across all schools.

Research indicates that early academic planning—particularly when structured and deliberate—supports higher student engagement and improved long-term outcomes. A systematic review published in Frontiers in Psychology (2025) confirms that middle school–based career interventions significantly enhance students' career decision-making skills and adaptability. Notably, the study identified counselor support as the most critical factor influencing the effectiveness of these programs (Wang & Wang, 2025).

Additionally, a policy report by ACT emphasizes that beginning postsecondary planning in middle school enables students to choose high school courses more strategically, increasing their chances of completing rigorous programs and graduating on time (ACT, Inc., n.d.).

High School Counselors:
Balancing Readiness, Support, and Pressure

As students progress to high school, the role of the school counselor becomes more layered and intensive. The responsibilities expand significantly compared to earlier grade levels, reflecting the complexity of student needs at this stage. High school counselors are expected to provide direct support in three primary areas: academic planning, college and career readiness, and mental health. Their ability to do this effectively depends on the structure of their counseling program and whether it is aligned with the American School Counselor Association (ASCA) National Model or a corresponding state framework.

The ASCA National Model emphasizes a comprehensive approach that balances academic, social-emotional, and postsecondary development. Counselors in high schools help students understand graduation requirements, prepare for standardized testing, identify career paths, and apply to colleges, trade schools, or workforce opportunities. These tasks are often supported by tools such as career inventories, college-planning platforms, and structured advising sessions. States that follow the ASCA model tend to provide similar tools, although variations in access and support services can affect student outcomes. In under-resourced districts, counselors may have large caseloads that limit their ability to provide individualized support.

Beyond academic planning, high school students face emotional and social pressures that include anxiety related to grades, peer relationships, identity development, and future uncertainty. Counselors provide a critical layer of mental health support by offering one-on-one counseling, small group sessions, and referrals to outside services when needed. Many states have added mental health components to their models to match this growing demand. The ASCA model supports this need through clearly defined competencies in emotional regulation and coping skills.

Counselors also address common high school issues such as academic stress, test anxiety, and college admissions pressure. They help students balance extracurricular activities, part-time work, and personal responsibilities. For those experiencing family conflict or economic hardship, counselors often act as a bridge to community resources or school-based support teams. In many cases, they serve as the only consistent point of contact between students, families, and educators. This holistic engagement is essential in promoting student well-being and achievement.

A survey of secondary school counselors found that many are burdened with heavy workloads, including administrative tasks, leaving less time for direct student support. Counselors expressed strong support for introducing stepped-care, web-based mental health services to improve efficiency, allow earlier detection of issues, and reduce personal burnout (O'Dea et al., 2017).

The Value of Continuity and Collaboration in Counseling Services

A key aspect of effective school counseling is the continuity of support that students receive across all grade levels. From the early elementary years to high school graduation, students experience a wide range of developmental, academic, and emotional changes. Continuity in counseling ensures that each student receives appropriate support during these transitions. It also allows for the development of long-term strategies that are responsive to each student's evolving needs. When counseling services are coordinated across elementary, middle, and high school, students benefit from a consistent structure that helps them stay on track academically and emotionally.

The ASCA National Model encourages school systems to view counseling as a developmental process, which means that services should not operate in isolation by grade level, but rather build upon each other to support the whole child. For example, early exposure to emotional regulation and peer relationships in elementary school lays the groundwork for more advanced skills in conflict resolution, academic planning, and postsecondary decision-making in later years. When schools adopt this framework and apply it consistently, students are more likely to feel connected, supported, and prosperous in their academic journey. In contrast, state-level models may vary in their commitment to seamless K-12 integration, depending on funding, staffing, and training mandates.

One of the most important ways to ensure continuity is through collaboration. School counselors play a central role in bringing together teachers, parents, and support staff to create comprehensive support plans. School counselors play a key role in leading Student Support Teams. They help coordinate regular meetings where team members discuss intervention strategies and work together to improve school culture and climate. When a student struggles either academically or emotionally, the counselor coordinates with classroom teachers to monitor performance and implement in-class strategies. At the same time, counselors engage families in ongoing conversations about their child's needs, ensuring that home and school environments are aligned in their approach. This joint effort results in Individualized Support Plans or targeted interventions that help students make progress while building resilience.

Recent scholarship highlights the indispensable role school counselors play in orchestrating student support efforts through collaboration with educators, families, and support staff. A 2023 qualitative study focusing on counselor–teacher partnerships for multilingual learners underscores how effective collaboration enables informed decision-making based on student needs and identities, further positioning counselors as essential problem solvers and leaders within schools (Davis et al., 2023).

Additionally, a study on parents' expectations of counselors found that forging transparent, trust-based relationships between counselors and caregivers strengthens home–school collaboration. The findings suggest that clear communication and shared understanding improve mental health outcomes for students and enhance school-wide wellbeing strategies (Collins et al., 2024).

Together, these insights affirm that school counselors are far more than individual support providers; they are central connectors whose coordination of Student Support Teams and alliance with teachers and parents cultivates individualized intervention plans and promotes a cohesive, student-centered school climate.

Counselors at each level use tools such as student assessments, behavior reports, and academic data to inform these plans. They also schedule regular meetings with stakeholders to review student progress and revise strategies as needed. These collaborative practices ensure that support is not reactive, but proactive and continuous. In schools where counselors are fully integrated into the academic and emotional planning processes, students are less likely to fall through the cracks. They also develop stronger relationships with adults who understand their personal histories and are better equipped to guide them over time.

Although many states encourage collaboration and continuity in their school counseling guidelines, implementation remains uneven. The ASCA model provides clear direction for best practices, but districts must ensure proper counselor-to-student ratios, access to data systems, and time for collaboration to make this possible. Without this support, counselors often face barriers that limit their ability to deliver consistent services.

Addressing Developmental Challenges
and Preventing Dropout Through Counseling

As students progress through the educational system, they encounter various challenges tied to their stage of development. School counselors play an important role in identifying these challenges early and responding with appropriate, structured support. Their involvement helps students build coping strategies, stay connected to learning, and make steady progress through each academic stage.

In elementary school, one of the most common concerns is social integration. Young children are learning how to form friendships, work cooperatively, and manage emotions for the first time in a school setting. Counselors guide students through these early social experiences by coaching core skills in emotional regulation, empathy, and communication. Structured group sessions and classroom presentations focused on social development can reduce isolation and bullying, helping children feel a stronger sense of belonging in school.

In middle school, students begin to face increased peer pressure, identity exploration, and academic expectations. This period often involves greater emotional intensity and a strong desire for acceptance. School counselors help students manage these hurdles by creating safe spaces to discuss personal concerns and develop decision-making skills. They also work with teachers to identify students showing signs of disengagement or stress. Middle school counselors are essential in promoting self-awareness and resilience, both of which are critical as students prepare for the demands of high school.

By the time students reach high school, the focus shifts toward post-secondary planning and academic achievement. Students face pressure related to grades, college applications, scholarships, and career choices. Counselors offer guidance on all of these topics while continuing to support students' emotional well-being. They help students balance academic goals with mental health needs and provide targeted interventions for those at risk of falling behind or dropping out.

Dropout prevention remains a key area where high school counselors can make a measurable difference. Research consistently shows that lower student-to-counselor ratios correlate with stronger academic outcomes and higher graduation rates, indicating that increased counselor access enhances student support.

A focused study in Texas reinforces this pattern, demonstrating that schools with more counselor support report better retention and academic success. These findings lend strong empirical support to the need for funding and policy alignment with the ASCA National Model by ensuring adequate staffing, structured interventions, and preventive programming. Counselors can more effectively address developmental needs and dropout risks at multiple levels (Brown & Knight, 2023).

In contrast, some state models may not offer clear direction or sufficient funding to support such comprehensive efforts. Variability in counselor-to-student ratios and inconsistent professional development contribute to unequal service delivery across districts. This gap reinforces the need to advocate for adherence to the ASCA National Model, which provides a reliable outline for addressing developmental needs and dropout risk at each level.

Integrating Counseling with Instructional Goals and Supporting Counselor Development

As the roles of school counselors continue to expand, it becomes increasingly important to align counseling programs with the broader instructional goals of schools. Social-emotional learning (SEL) should not be seen as a separate or secondary initiative. Instead, it must be integrated into the academic environment to support the whole student. When counseling efforts are coordinated with classroom instruction, students benefit from a more cohesive and supportive learning experience.

A meta-analysis of school counselor–led SEL interventions published in Journal of Counseling & Development (2024) found that when counselors deliver SEL programs, these interventions have a small to moderate positive effect on student outcomes (Hedges's $g \approx$ 0.308) This evidence underscores that counselor-facilitated SEL not only supports students' emotional and social development but also enhances academic engagement when integrated into the instructional environment (Van Velsor, 2009).

The ASCA National Model emphasizes the value of aligning school counseling programs with academic standards. It encourages counselors to collaborate with teachers and administrators in developing SEL initiatives that are embedded in classroom lessons. For example, when a counselor does a presentation on emotional regulation or conflict resolution in partnership with a language arts teacher, students have the opportunity to apply SEL principles while developing their communication and critical thinking skills. This kind of integration reinforces both academic and social growth.

In comparison, some state models provide partial guidance on how to connect counseling with instructional goals. This leads to a fragmented approach in many schools, where counselors may be viewed as peripheral to the core mission of teaching and learning. Without clear expectations and administrative support, the opportunity to fully embed SEL within academic instruction is often missed. As a result, the potential for stronger outcomes in both academic performance and student well-being is reduced.

To bridge this gap, ongoing professional development is essential. School counselors need to stay informed about emerging research, evolving student needs, and effective practices in SEL, trauma-informed care, equity, and college and career readiness. The ASCA model highlights the importance of continuous learning through training, conferences, and collaboration with professional networks. States that invest in structured professional development for counselors are better positioned to respond to current challenges such as increased anxiety, digital dependency, and post-pandemic learning gaps.

According to ASCA's position statements, school counselors are expected to "lead, advocate, and collaborate to promote equity and access," connecting their programs with district missions and school improvement efforts. This highlights how professional development in these areas, such as through training, conferences, and peer networks, activates the counselor's capacity to contribute meaningfully to systemic school goals (Reese, 2021).

Unfortunately, not all state models provide adequate funding or clear pathways for professional growth. In districts with limited resources, counselors may lack access to the training they need to remain effective and current. This further widens the disparity in support services among schools. To ensure consistent quality, all states must adopt comprehensive models aligned with ASCA's standards and allocate funding for professional development as a core component of school counseling programs.

Conclusion

Throughout all levels of education, from elementary to high school, school counselors serve as indispensable contributors to student success. Their work is most effective when aligned with academic goals and supported by strong professional development. The ASCA National Model offers a robust model that prioritizes data-informed decision-making, equitable access, and the integration of SEL into the educational experience. While many state models attempt to follow similar principles, gaps in implementation and support continue to limit their effectiveness. A consistent, nationally aligned approach ensures that all students, regardless of background or location, receive the guidance, support, and opportunities they need to thrive.

~∞

Chapter 4:
School Counselors and Leadership

The role of school is no longer confined to traditional responsibilities of scheduling, career advisement, or crisis response. School counselors are now recognized as integral leaders within school systems, and this evolving identity includes active participation in shaping school policies, leading systemic change, and ensuring student support frameworks are aligned with both academic and developmental goals. The American School Counselor Association (ASCA) National Model emphasizes this leadership role by positioning counselors as collaborative partners in comprehensive school reform efforts.

To fulfill the evolving role effectively, school counselors must possess and consistently develop a specific set of professional skills and personal qualities. Strong communication skills are fundamental, as counselors regularly interact with students, families, administrators, and staff to exchange critical information and advocate for student needs. Equally important are problem-solving abilities, which enable counselors to address individual concerns and make meaningful contributions to school-wide challenges.

Emotional intelligence and empathy are essential for understanding and responding appropriately to the emotional and social needs of diverse student populations. These traits also enable counselors to navigate sensitive conversations and promote a positive school climate. In addition, leadership and sound decision-making skills empower counselors to initiate, guide, and evaluate support initiatives that benefit the broader school community.

A 2022 study by Hilts et al. explored the relationship between school counselors' emotional intelligence (EI) and their capacity to lead and implement comprehensive school counseling programs (CSCP). The study, which involved 792 practicing school counselors, found that EI significantly predicted the use of transformational leadership ($r = .42$, $p < .001$). Furthermore, leadership practices mediated the relationship between EI and effective implementation of counseling programs, with an indirect effect of 0.15 ($p < .001$).

These findings highlight the critical role of emotional intelligence in helping counselors understand the diverse needs of students through empathy and emotional awareness, navigate sensitive conversations with students, staff, and families, and make informed decisions that align with both counseling program goals and broader school improvement priorities (Hilts, Liu, & Luke, 2022).

To carry out this work effectively, school counselors collaborate closely with administrators, teachers, and parents. With administrators, counselors contribute to the development of school improvement plans, help guide policy decisions, and offer recommendations that support student wellness alongside academic success. Their participation in school leadership and coordination teams ensures that student needs are consistently represented in strategic planning and resource allocation.

The ASCA model outlines this advocacy and systemic change function as essential for an all-embracing counseling program. By working across stakeholder groups, school counselors help shape school environments that are responsive, inclusive, and student-centered. Their ability to lead these efforts through strong relationships, informed insight, and evidence-based strategies underscores the growing importance of their role in systemic school change.

Counselors are uniquely equipped to bring the student perspective into broader school conversations. Their daily work places them in close contact with students from diverse backgrounds, allowing them to identify emerging needs and trends that may not be visible through academic data alone. Through this lens, they can advocate for inclusive policies, culturally responsive practices, and interventions that reduce barriers to success. For instance, school counselors often champion initiatives on equity in course placement, access to advanced coursework, or the development of positive behavioral frameworks.

Effective collaboration is also key. With administrators, counselors help shape school improvement plans, inform policy decisions, and ensure that student wellness is integrated into strategic goals. Teachers identify students needing academic or social-emotional support and coordinate interventions like peer mediation, behavior plans, or accommodations. This collaboration ensures that educators consider the full scope of student needs.

Engaging families is another cornerstone of a counselor's leadership. Acting as a bridge between home and school, counselors support parents in navigating educational systems and accessing services. They lead or participate in conferences, support team meetings, and special education planning, fostering a shared commitment to student well-being.

The ASCA model frames advocacy and systemic change as essential components of comprehensive counseling programs. By working across stakeholder groups and employing evidence-based strategies, school counselors help create inclusive, responsive, and student-centered school environments—highlighting their critical role in educational leadership.

Building a Comprehensive Counseling Program Aligned with School Goals

A strong school counseling program must be rooted in the overall vision and mission of the school. This connection ensures that the work of the counselor contributes directly to the academic, social, and emotional development of every student. The American School Counselor Association (ASCA) National Model supports this by outlining a framework in which counseling programs are intentional, measurable, and wholly integrated into the broader educational system. While many state models reflect this same foundation, the consistency of implementation often depends on local leadership, available resources, and policy alignment.

Establishing a wide-ranging program begins with a clear understanding of schoolwide goals. School counselors contribute to this process by using data to identify student needs and proposing strategies that support academic success, positive behavior, and emotional resilience. When aligned effectively, counseling goals reflect the broader goals of the school and offer added support that promotes students' academic progress along with their social, emotional, and mental well-being. This alignment makes the counselor a valued contributor to school planning and decision-making processes.

A recent position statement by the American School Counselor Association (ASCA) emphasizes that school counselors are responsible for designing and implementing comprehensive programs that are closely aligned with their school's vision, mission, and goals. These programs are grounded in data-informed decision-making and aim to enhance student academic achievement. ASCA highlights that effective school counseling programs use data—and specifically disaggregated data—to identify the unique needs of diverse student populations.

This approach enables counselors to provide targeted interventions and advocate for equitable access to coursework and support services. In doing so, school counselors actively work to eliminate systemic barriers, ensuring that all students have the opportunity to meet their full academic potential (Goodman-Scott, Betters-Bubon, & Donohue, 2015).

A well-developed program is not only proactive in structure but also flexible enough to respond to evolving student needs. For example, while the ASCA model emphasizes core components such as individual planning, responsive services, and system support, state models may adjust these areas to better reflect local priorities. Comparing national and state-level approaches reveals opportunities for strengthening the connections between policy and practice.

Advocating for student needs is also central to broader program development. School counselors are in a key position to speak on behalf of students who may not otherwise be heard. This includes supporting those who face social, emotional, or academic challenges and promoting equitable access to programs and resources. Strategies such as disaggregating data by student group, collaborating with families and staff, and ensuring inclusive practices can lead to better outcomes for all learners. For example, some counselors have led efforts to revise school policies that disproportionately affect students of color by presenting data on suspension rates and advocating for restorative justice practices. Others have implemented targeted interventions for English language learners by coordinating with ESL staff and creating support groups that address language and transition challenges.

Counselors also work to create school environments where students feel safe, valued, and understood. This requires ongoing collaboration with administrators, educators, and support staff. Through partnerships, school counselors help shape practices that remove barriers to learning and promote belonging. One such example is the implementation of peer mentorship programs in middle schools, where older students are paired with younger students to promote connection and reduce bullying. In another case, high school counselors partnered with families and community agencies to host mental health workshops, increasing access to culturally responsive services and reducing stigma.

In states where counselor programs are closely modeled after ASCA standards, schools tend to show higher levels of student engagement and positive school climate. A 2023 peer-reviewed article in the *Journal of School-Based Counseling Policy and Evaluation* examined barriers to implementing the ASCA National Model across an entire state and highlighted a significant finding: schools formally aligned with ASCA standards—particularly those that have earned the

RAMP (Recognized ASCA Model Program) designation—consistently report higher levels of student engagement and more positive school climate compared to non-aligned schools.

This research emphasizes that when states adopt and actively support ASCA-aligned counseling programs, incorporating data-driven practices, equity-focused advocacy, and systemic planning, schools see not only academic improvements but also enhanced student connection, respect, and motivation. These findings affirm that fidelity to the ASCA model contributes meaningfully to the creation of inclusive and supportive school environments (Larberg & Sherlin, 2021).

Advocacy Through Collaboration and Leadership

School counselors play an essential role in advocating for students' needs by working closely with administrators, teachers, and families. This collaboration helps create an inclusive and supportive school environment where every student can access the resources necessary to thrive. The American School Counselor Association (ASCA) National Model supports this approach by outlining clear responsibilities for counselors in the areas of advocacy, leadership, and systemic change. Many state-level counseling frameworks also emphasize collaboration as a strategy to improve student outcomes and promote equity.

One of the most effective ways school counselors advocate for students is by facilitating open communication between all members of the school community. When counselors engage with teachers and administrators regularly, they can identify academic or emotional barriers early and recommend targeted strategies. This may involve reviewing data on student performance, attendance, or behavior and proposing intervention plans that support individual needs. In some cases, school counselors coordinate team meetings that include parents and other support personnel to ensure a full understanding of the student's circumstances.

Creating a supportive environment also means promoting inclusive practices that respect students from all backgrounds. School counselors can guide staff in recognizing cultural differences, supporting students with disabilities, and responding to the needs of English language learners.

A conceptual analysis published in *Frontiers in Education* argues that school counselors must integrate leadership, advocacy, collaboration, and systemic change to support inclusive, equitable access for students of color with disabilities. The study emphasizes that culturally responsive counseling ensures these students can succeed within general education, highlighting the counselor's role in guiding staff to recognize cultural differences and meet diverse student needs (Reese, 2021).

In schools that adopt the ASCA National Model, equity efforts are often embedded within a clearly structured and data-informed counseling program. This framework supports intentional planning and documentation, making equity goals measurable and sustainable. In addition to the ASCA model, frameworks such as the *Multi-Tiered System of Supports (MTSS)* and *Comprehensive School Counseling Programs (CSCPs)*, as outlined by state departments of education (e.g., the Texas Model for Comprehensive School Counseling Programs), also guide counselors in promoting access, opportunity, and fair treatment for all students.

Research by Hatch and Chen-Hayes (2008) emphasizes the need for school counselors to integrate equity-focused goals into their practice using outcome data to close achievement and opportunity gaps. Furthermore, the Education Trust's National Center for Transforming School Counseling has developed tools and training that support equity leadership among counselors, particularly in high-poverty schools.

These models, in combination, equip school counselors with practical tools to advocate for underrepresented student groups, disaggregate academic and behavioral data, and collaborate with school leaders to drive systemic change. As a result, schools using such frameworks report higher student participation in rigorous coursework, improved school climate measures, and stronger family engagement—critical indicators of equitable access and outcomes.

In addition to working within the school building, counselors are encouraged to assume leadership roles in the broader educational community. Participation in professional organizations, such as state school counselor associations or ASCA itself, helps counselors stay informed about current research, trends, and legislative developments. Many also serve on local education committees or advisory boards, contributing to decisions that shape school policy and practice.

Community outreach is another area where counselors can actively contribute. By building partnerships with local agencies, mental health providers, and nonprofit organizations, school counselors help connect students and families with additional services. These connections are especially important in under-resourced communities, where school counselors may be among the few professionals available to support students' non-academic needs.

Policy advocacy also remains a key area of leadership. School counselors can use their voice to influence legislation and funding decisions that affect counseling services at the local, state, and national levels. For example, by sharing data on student needs and program outcomes with school boards or policymakers, counselors can advocate for reduced student-to-counselor ratios and improved access to services.

Through consistent collaboration, active community engagement, and ongoing professional leadership, school counselors fulfill their role as both student advocates and systems change agents. When aligned with national and state frameworks, these efforts strengthen the counseling profession and ensure that all students are better supported in reaching their complete potential.

The Role of Data-Driven Practices and Leadership in Advancing School Counseling

Evidence-based approaches have become essential in demonstrating the effectiveness of school counseling programs and advocating for their expansion within educational systems. The American School Counselor Association (ASCA) National Model emphasizes the use of data to assess student needs, monitor progress, and evaluate outcomes. By collecting and analyzing data related to attendance, behavior, academic performance, and social-emotional development, school counselors can provide clear evidence of their impact on student success. This evidence is critical not only for guiding interventions but also for securing funding and support from school administrators and policymakers.

Many state counseling models incorporate data collection requirements aligned with the ASCA framework, although the extent of data use varies significantly across districts. Some states have developed sophisticated data management systems to help counselors track student progress and program results, while others rely on more informal methods. Despite these differences, the common goal remains: to establish measurable outcomes that validate counseling services as vital components of the school environment.

A 2023 study by Parzych, Generali, and Yavuz in the *Journal of Education* examined state-level variations in school counseling data systems and their alignment with the ASCA National Model. The study found that districts with formal data-management infrastructures—such as integrated dashboards and regular data reviews—enabled counselors to more effectively track student progress, measure program outcomes, and advocate for resources. Conversely, in districts without such systems, counselors relied more on informal tracking methods, which limited their ability to demonstrate measurable impact. Despite these differences, the study emphasized the shared objective: *"to establish measurable outcomes that validate counseling services as vital components of the school environment."* (Parzych, Generali, & Yavuz, 2021).

Strong leadership within the school counseling profession is closely linked to the ability to implement data-informed practices effectively. School counselors who assume leadership roles can influence school culture, advocate for systemic changes, and promote the integration of counseling services into the broader educational mission. Leadership involves not only managing a far-reaching counseling program but also collaborating with other stakeholders to align counseling goals with school priorities.

Research indicates that schools with counselors in leadership positions tend to have better student outcomes, including higher graduation rates, improved attendance, and reduced disciplinary referrals (Carey & Harrington, 2010). These positive results arise when counselors use data to identify needs, develop targeted interventions, and adjust strategies based on outcomes. Furthermore, visible leadership helps elevate the status of the counseling profession, making it clear that counselors contribute far beyond individual student support—they drive school-wide improvements.

The ASCA National Model promotes leadership through defined roles such as program coordinator, advocate, consultant, and collaborator. State models often reflect these roles, though resource availability affects how they can be realized. For instance, some states provide dedicated leadership training for counselors, while others offer limited professional development. Investing in leadership capacity is essential for advancing counseling programs and fostering recognition among educators and policymakers.

Moreover, leadership in school counseling extends beyond the school building to engagement with district administration, community partners, and legislative bodies. By presenting data-supported outcomes and championing the role of counseling in student development, counselors influence policies and resource allocation. This advocacy ensures that counseling remains a priority in educational planning and funding decisions.

Challenges Faced by School Counselors in Leadership Roles

School counselors operate within an increasingly complex and demanding educational environment. The aftermath of the recent pandemic has further intensified the mental health challenges faced by students, placing heightened demands on school counselors to provide support across social, emotional, academic, and career domains—all while working with limited resources.

Alexander, Savitz-Romer, Nicola, and Carroll (2022) conducted a mixed-methods study exploring how the COVID-19 pandemic intensified students' social, emotional, and mental health challenges, particularly among marginalized groups. Published in *Professional School Counseling*, the study highlights that school counselors became essential frontline support for students navigating anxiety, isolation, grief, and other pandemic-related mental health crises. However, despite their critical role, counselors faced significant barriers that limited their effectiveness.

These included overwhelming workloads, expanded responsibilities beyond traditional counseling, and a lack of institutional and organizational support. The study further revealed that counselors were expected to simultaneously address students' academic, social-emotional, career, and crisis-related needs. In addition, many were burdened with procedural tasks like attendance tracking and administrative communication, while also transitioning to virtual service delivery, all of which reduced the time and resources available for direct student engagement.

These findings underscore the growing demands placed on school counselors in a post-pandemic educational landscape and the urgent need for systemic support to enable them to fulfill their multifaceted role effectively.

One of the significant challenges counselors face is navigating school systems that may lack a clear understanding or support for their role. Balancing the broad needs of students with administrative responsibilities requires strong leadership, clear communication, and the ability to collaborate effectively with instructional staff and school administrators (Dollarhide & Saginak, 2017). These demands are compounded by the rapid pace of societal change, which requires school counselors to stay informed of current best practices and to apply evidence-based interventions in their daily work (Hatch & Shuttleworth, 2016).

Unfortunately, there remains a widespread lack of understanding among school communities regarding the comprehensive role of school counselors. Many stakeholders are unaware of how counselors contribute to the holistic development of students—supporting their academic progress, emotional well-being, and future planning. This limited awareness can result in a lack of recognition and underutilization of the counseling role (Hatch & Shuttleworth, 2016).

As expectations continue to rise, school counselors are asked to do more with fewer resources. They are expected to respond to complex student needs, support school-wide initiatives, and manage ever-expanding responsibilities. To meet these demands effectively, school counselors must engage in continuous professional development, strengthen their advocacy skills, and maintain open lines of communication with students, staff, and families.

Investing in these areas not only enhances individual counselor effectiveness but also reinforces the impact of comprehensive school counseling programs. When counselors are empowered with the tools, knowledge, and support they need, they are better positioned to contribute meaningfully to student success and the overall well-being of the school community in today's evolving society.

The Role of Mentorship in Developing Leadership Among School Counselors

Professional support plays a vital role in cultivating guidance expertise among school counselors, providing essential support for both new and experienced professionals. As the field of school counseling continues to evolve, the need for effective directional influence has become increasingly apparent. Experienced counselors, through mentorship, serve as guides who help emerging counselors build the confidence, knowledge, and skills necessary to assume coordinating roles within their schools and districts.

A 2024 peer-reviewed study in the *School Counselor* journal offers strong support for your point. Researchers examined the induction and mentoring experiences of early-career school counselors and found clear benefits: "Induction programs, particularly mentoring, positively impact beginning counselors' job satisfaction and retention."

These findings highlight how both formal and informal mentoring arrangements—where experienced counselors share their insights and provide guidance—play a vital role in professional growth. Such mentor partnerships help new counselors acclimate to school systems, develop confidence, and enhance their capacity to take on oversight responsibilities. This evidence aligns directly with the ASCA National Model's emphasis on mentorship as a strategic tool for building leadership competence and effective counseling programs (Kitching et al., 2024).

The American School Counselor Association (ASCA) National Model recognizes peer development as a key strategy to develop capacity for oversight within the profession. This model encourages the establishment of formal and informal mentoring relationships, where seasoned counselors share their expertise and insights on navigating school systems, advocating for students, and collaborating with educators and administrators. These relationships foster professional growth by offering new counselors practical advice, emotional support, and constructive feedback that are critical for success in supervisory responsibilities.

State counseling models vary in their approach to mentorship programs. Some states have formal guidance initiatives embedded within their counselor preparation or induction programs, while others leave this support largely to individual districts or voluntary arrangements. The availability and structure of coaching can greatly influence how quickly new counselors adapt to the demands of their roles and how effectively they develop leadership competencies. States that align closely with the ASCA National Model often provide clearer guidance and resources for mentorship, emphasizing its importance in building a strong counseling workforce.

Mentorship benefits extend beyond the development of individual counselors; it also strengthens the overall counseling program by promoting continuity and consistency. Experienced counselors help mentees understand the broader goals of inclusive school counseling programs, including the use of data to inform practice, advocacy for student needs, and active participation in school management. This collegial support enables new counselors to align their work with district and state priorities, which enhances program effectiveness and the recognition of counseling as a critical component of the educational system.

Additionally, mentorship addresses challenges commonly faced by new counselors, such as feeling isolated or uncertain about their roles. By fostering a supportive professional community, mentors help mentees build networks that encourage collaboration and ongoing learning. This support is particularly important in states or districts where resources are limited, and counselors may work with high caseloads and multiple demands.

The Importance of Professional Development for School Counselors in Leadership Roles

Professional development and clinical supervision are essential components in ensuring the effectiveness of school counselors and the overall success of school counseling programs. Ongoing professional development enables counselors to refine their competencies, remain informed about emerging trends, and apply evidence-based strategies in addressing students' academic, social, emotional, and career-related needs. It also fosters collaboration, offering opportunities for school counselors to connect with peers, share insights, and build professional networks that enhance their practice.

Equally important is the role of supervision, particularly when guided by experienced professionals with a strong foundation in school counseling. Supervision provides a structured and reflective space where counselors can review their work, receive constructive feedback, and navigate complex cases with support. It reinforces ethical standards, encourages personal and professional growth, and helps counselors manage the emotional demands of their role through self-care and accountability.

Effective supervision plays a vital role in both the professional development of school counselors and the overall consistency and quality of services provided to students. Bernard and Goodyear (2019) emphasize that supervision enhances counselor competencies, sharpens decision-making, and reinforces professional standards, ultimately increasing confidence and aligning counselors more closely with educational goals.

Additionally, a recent mixed-methods study utilizing the School Counseling Supervision Model (SCSM) found that structured group supervision led to measurable improvements in the fidelity of counseling practices and the consistency of student services (Bernard & Luke, 2020).

These findings demonstrate that when school counselors receive purposeful and ongoing supervision, they are better equipped to provide effective, equitable, and high-quality support. Such supervision not only benefits the individual counselor but also strengthens their role within the broader educational system, ensuring that students receive reliable and informed guidance aligned with district and state expectations.

By prioritizing both professional development and supervision, school systems can enhance the impact of their counseling programs. This investment leads to stronger service delivery, improved student outcomes, and a healthier, more resilient school community where counselors are empowered to lead and support students with confidence and clarity.

Reflections on the Future of School Counseling Leadership

The future of school counseling leadership depends heavily on the profession's ability to maintain strong advocacy efforts, foster professional collaboration, and adapt continuously to the evolving needs of students and educational systems. As school counselors take on more expansive roles within schools, they must remain proactive drivers of change who not only respond to current challenges but also anticipate future demands.

The American School Counselor Association (ASCA) National Model provides a clear framework for the ongoing development of guidance within the profession. It encourages counselors to engage actively in shaping school policies, promoting equity and inclusion, and integrating social-emotional well-being alongside academic goals. State models vary in how closely they align with the ASCA model, with some adopting comprehensive management expectations for counselors while others emphasize more traditional roles. These differences can affect the readiness of counselors to lead effectively and advocate for necessary changes in their schools.

Continued advocacy remains a cornerstone of advancing the field. School counselors must champion their role as vital contributors to student success and well-being. This includes advocating for adequate staffing, sufficient resources, and the integration of counseling programs within the school's overall mission. Tactful leadership helps elevate the perception of school counseling from a support service to a strategic partner in education. Effective advocacy is supported by outcome-focused evidence that demonstrates the positive impact of counseling on academic achievement, mental health, and school climate.

Professional collaboration is equally important. School counselors do not work in isolation; their leadership is most effective when it involves building strong partnerships with administrators, teachers, families, and community organizations. Collaborative efforts ensure that counseling initiatives are integrated into broader educational strategies and that students receive consistent support across different environments. State models that encourage collaboration and multidisciplinary teamwork tend to produce more cohesive and effective counseling programs.

Adaptability is essential as students' needs continue to evolve due to social changes, technological advances, and emerging mental health concerns. The demands placed on school counselors are increasingly complex, requiring leaders who are flexible and willing to embrace new approaches. This may include adopting trauma-informed practices, addressing digital citizenship, or expanding outreach to underserved populations. Leadership development programs and ongoing professional learning opportunities are crucial to preparing counselors for these challenges.

Looking forward, the role of school counseling leadership will expand beyond traditional boundaries. Counselors will need to be visible advocates within their schools and communities, skilled collaborators who bridge gaps among stakeholders, and innovative thinkers who guide programs responsive to the future educational landscape. State models that align closely with the ASCA National Model offer a strong foundation for developing these capacities, but continuous refinement and resource support remain necessary.

In conclusion, the future of school counseling leadership lies in a commitment to sustained advocacy, meaningful collaboration, and ongoing adaptation. By embracing these principles, school counselors can ensure their profession remains vital and effective in supporting the holistic development of all students. Comparing state models to the national framework reveals areas of strength and opportunities for growth that will shape the trajectory of school counseling in the years to come.

While the ASCA National Model is a valuable and widely recognized framework for validating the role of school counselors, it is important to diversify the sources used to support the various ideas presented. Relying heavily on ASCA alone can limit the perspective and depth of the discussion. Incorporating additional evidence-based research, state-level models, and insights from educational leadership, psychology, and social work literature can provide a more well-rounded understanding of the evolving role of school counselors. Broadening the range of sources strengthens the credibility of the content and highlights the multidimensional nature of school counseling practice.

Chapter 5:
Challenges and Hurdles in School Counseling

Ambiguous Professional Identity & Role Overload

School counselors often grapple with undefined roles and fragmented responsibilities, which hinder their ability to serve students effectively.

A 2020 study in *Sociology of Education* reports that counselors in high schools suffer from role ambiguity and role conflict due to vague job descriptions, overlapping duties with other staff, supervision from non-counseling administrators, and inadequate performance evaluation systems. This misalignment shifts their focus away from providing social-emotional and academic support, relegating them to administrative functions instead of leveraging their expertise in student development (Hannor-Walker et al., 2022).

Role stress—comprising ambiguity, conflict, and overload— further exacerbates the problem. A study published in the

International Journal of Environmental Research and Public Health, which describes counselor experiences during the pandemic, highlights that counselors frequently encountered multiple conflicting expectations, unclear responsibilities, and excessive workloads, all of which significantly impacted their well-being and efficacy (Alexander et al., 2022).

This aligns with findings in *The Professional Counselor*, where educators noted that administrative overload, including testing coordination, paperwork, and Section 504 duties, prevented them from dedicating at least 80% of their time to direct student services. One counselor described spending "90 percent on paperwork and not building relationships with kids," emphasizing how role overload erodes the counselor's true purpose: supporting students (Blake, 2020).

Implications & Professional Significance

- **Reduced effectiveness**: When counselors are diverted to non-counseling tasks, opportunities for preventive intervention, relationship-building, and meaningful student support are diminished.

- **Strained supervision**: Without proper direction from trained counseling leaders, counselors remain unsure of expectations—limiting their growth and efficacy.

- **Fragmented support**: Lacking cohesive frameworks and professional clarity, counseling efforts become isolated actions—what some researchers term *"random acts of guidance."*

- **Impact on morale**: Persistent role overload and ambiguity contribute to heightened stress and burnout, reducing job satisfaction and potentially limiting service quality and longevity in the field.

Excessive Caseloads & Administrative Burdens

School counselors across the United States continue to manage caseloads that significantly exceed recommended professional standards. The American School Counselor Association (ASCA) recommends a student-to-counselor ratio of 250:1, yet many districts report numbers far exceeding this benchmark. According to the 2025 School Counselor Report, 56% of counselors serve between 300 and 400 students, while others exceed even that threshold (YouScience, 2025).

In some urban areas, the disparities are more pronounced. For example, Houston ISD counselors have a ratio of 1 counselor for every 476 students, which exceeds ASCA's recommendation and limits their ability to provide individualized planning, mental health support, or career readiness guidance (Houston Chronicle, 2025).

The impact of these inflated caseloads is far-reaching. Counselors with large student rosters must often prioritize crisis intervention and administrative tasks over proactive, developmentally appropriate programming. This results in a reactive counseling model where preventive efforts, such as social-emotional learning workshops or career exploration sessions, are reduced or overlooked entirely. Ultimately, students receive unequal access to essential counseling services, particularly in underfunded districts where ratios are most extreme.

Administrative Tasks Take Precedence over Counseling

In addition to large caseloads, school counselors face the burden of excessive administrative responsibilities. A majority of counselors report that compliance-related duties and clerical tasks account for nearly half of their working hours (YouScience, 2025). These tasks include coordinating standardized tests, scheduling, data entry, and completing paperwork related to accountability reporting. While these functions are important, they detract from the counselor's core role of providing academic, career, and social-emotional guidance.

Research indicates that a combination of high caseloads and non-counseling responsibilities contributes significantly to school counselor burnout and diminished job satisfaction. For example, Mullen et al. (2021) conducted a cross-sectional survey of 327 school counselors, finding that larger student caseloads were associated with increased burnout and job stress, as well as decreased job satisfaction.

These stressors compromise counselors' capacity to form meaningful connections with students and reduce the effectiveness of school-wide counseling initiatives. In effect, role overload prevents counselors from fulfilling the very mission for which they are employed.

Implications for Student Outcomes

The implications of excessive caseloads and administrative overload extend beyond the well-being of counselors. Students in schools with higher counselor-to-student ratios report less access to individualized academic planning, fewer career readiness opportunities, and limited mental health support. Goodman-Scott, Sink, Cholewa, and Burgess (2018) conducted a comprehensive study titled "An Ecological View of School Counselor Ratios and Student Academic Outcomes: A National Investigation".

Published in the Journal of Counseling & Development, this research analyzed data from the 2009 High School Longitudinal Study, a representative national dataset. The study found that student-to-counselor ratios were significantly associated with student GPA and high school graduation rates. Schools with more favorable ratios achieved notably better academic outcomes.

Mental Health Demands Outpace Preparedness

Student mental health has become a significant concern for school counselors across the nation. A recent survey of K–12 school counselors found that 94% agree schools cannot manage the youth mental health crisis effectively at Tier 3 intervention levels alone, and that mental health support is a primary demand on their services (Catapult Learning, 2025). However, many counselors report feeling underprepared to meet these escalating needs. A significant majority struggle to deliver consistent support, often facing limited time, insufficient tools, and growing personal stress as a direct consequence.

Stigma as a Barrier in Minority Communities

At the same time, cultural stigma and distrust surrounding mental health persist—adding layers of complexity to delivering support. A comprehensive systematic review of mental health stigma among ethnic minority groups in the United States found that racial and ethnic minorities often experience greater public, self-, and structural stigma compared to White Americans. Common themes included fears of being seen as a burden to the family, lack of community awareness, and negative internal attitudes toward mental illness (Misra et al., 2021).

Implications for Practice

- **Counselor Training Needs Intensify:** The gap between demand and readiness highlights the critical necessity of increased training in trauma-informed care, crisis intervention, and culturally responsive practice.

- **Stigma Reduction Requires Strategy:** Addressing deep-seated stigma will involve outreach, transparent communication, trust-building with families, and culturally informed support frameworks—particularly for minority students who may face dual stigma from both mental health and cultural perspectives.

- **Equity in Counseling Access:** Without systemic support, counselors may be constrained in serving the most vulnerable students—those facing mental health needs in communities impacted by stigma or limited resources.

Lack of Supervision, Mentorship & Professional Support:

- **Operating in Isolation** Many school counselors work with minimal professional oversight or structured mentorship, leaving them to navigate demanding roles independently. A mixed-methods study highlighted that counselors who perceive low levels of organizational or supervisory support are significantly more likely to experience burnout, emotional exhaustion, and reduced professional satisfaction. These counselors also report decreased job autonomy and increased intention to turnover (Duncan et al., 2014).

- **Mentorship Gaps Especially Impact Novices:** The value of mentorship in counselor development is well documented, yet access remains inconsistent. Research among rural, certified school counselors found that regular clinical supervision and peer consultation are critical for skill development, reflective practice, and resilience-building. However, many did not receive such structured support, which negatively impacted their professional confidence and efficacy (Bardhoshi et al., 2014).

- **Impact on Well-Being and Retention:** Without regular supervision or mentorship, counselors face heightened role ambiguity and are unable to fully benefit from professional feedback, which is vital for their growth. Evidence suggests that a lack of supportive mentoring and supervision exacerbates stress and burnout, thereby increasing the likelihood that counselors will either leave the profession or reduce the quality of their services. Clear supervisory structures and professional guidance serve as a protective resource, bolstering resilience and retention.

Challenges in Measuring Impact & Securing Funding

- **Measuring the Effectiveness of Counseling Programs:** Assessing the actual impact of school counseling remains a persistent challenge due to the complex nature of student growth. Quantitative measures often fail to capture improvements in social-emotional learning, coping skills, or resilience. A recent mixed-methods evaluation revealed that students engaged with counseling programs showed increased academic performance and a 10% higher attendance rate compared to peers who did not participate (Simbolon & Purba, 2022). This study also noted that such holistic gains are difficult to measure with standardized tools—reinforcing the importance of qualitative feedback alongside numeric data.

- **Funding Shortfalls Undermine Counseling Service:** Budget constraints pose a significant threat to the potential of school counseling programs. A May 2024 report from the National Center for Education Statistics (NCES) found that 55% of public schools struggle due to insufficient mental health staff, and 54% cite inadequate funding as a significant barrier to providing adequate student support. Notably, only 48% of schools reported that they could adequately serve all students' mental health needs—down from 56% just two years earlier (NCES, 2024). The reduction in federal and local funding—often used to sustain counseling positions—forces districts to make cuts that limit access to these essential services

Implications for Practice

- **Invisible Impact, Visible Need**: Counseling often yields qualitative outcomes, including improved resilience and enhanced emotional regulation. These are difficult to quantify, which makes advocating for funding more difficult in environments driven by test scores and attendance metrics.

- **Resource Gaps Exacerbate Inequity:** Schools with limited budgets must make difficult choices, and counseling services often face cuts, particularly in under-resourced districts, which intensifies inequities in student support.

- **Call for Multi-faceted Evaluation:** A blended approach that combines data (such as attendance and grades) with narrative accounts and case studies can more accurately reflect the benefits of counseling programs.

- **Urgent Funding Advocacy Required:** Without steady investment, schools cannot maintain the infrastructure necessary for sustainable counseling services. Counselors and education leaders must advocate strategically for funding that reflects the profession's long-term value.

Conclusion

The challenges facing school counselors are significant and multifaceted, ranging from unclear professional roles and excessive caseloads to underfunded programs and limited supervision. Counselors are increasingly expected to provide academic guidance, mental health support, and systemic leadership; yet, they often lack the resources and structural support necessary to succeed in these areas. High caseloads and administrative burdens diminish their ability to engage directly with students, while inadequate professional development and supervision contribute to stress and attrition.

Further, persistent stigma around mental health and inequities in funding complicate efforts to deliver consistent and equitable services. These obstacles underscore the need for robust frameworks, sufficient funding, and transparent accountability measures to ensure that school counselors can effectively address the evolving and complex needs of today's students. Addressing these barriers is not only critical to the effectiveness of counseling programs but also essential to the long-term success and well-being of students in diverse educational settings.

⌒◯

Chapter 6:
Social, Emotional,
and Academic Development

Link Between Emotional Well-Being
and Academic Success

Emotional well-being, social–emotional competencies, and academic development are deeply intertwined. A recent large-scale study of over 215,000 Australian students (Years 4 to 10) found that emotional well-being, engagement, and learning readiness—defined as perseverance, confidence, and focus—are vital predictors of academic performance on standardized tests such as NAPLAN and PAT. The research emphasized that emotional health is not simply an adjunct to academic skills but rather shapes a student's preparedness and ability to learn effectively (University of South Australia, 2025).

Further, an international longitudinal investigation among undergraduate students revealed that impaired mental health at the start of university significantly increased the risk of poorer academic performance over four years. Notably, this relationship persisted even when accounting for lifestyle factors, including diet, sleep, and exercise. The findings underscore that emotional well-being serves as a foundational condition for sustained academic achievement over time (Chu et al., 2023).

Together, these studies suggest a clear pattern: students who are emotionally supported and mentally healthy demonstrate stronger engagement, greater resilience in learning, and ultimately better academic outcomes. Emotional well-being thus functions as a critical foundation for performance and student success.

Counselors' Role in Skill Development

School counselors play a central role in cultivating students' emotional intelligence, self-regulation, and conflict-resolution skills, all of which support academic success.

In one empirical study, elementary students who participated in structured emotional-intelligence counseling showed significant improvements in self-control, resilience, and constructive conflict management, with teachers reporting notably fewer impulsive behaviors and more harmonious peer interactions (Syahrul et al., 2025).

At the secondary and professional level, counselors' capacity for emotional intelligence also supports effective program implementation. A national survey of 792 practicing school counselors found that higher emotional-intelligence scores correlated positively with their use of transformational leadership and the effectiveness of comprehensive school counseling programs (CSCP).

Emotional intelligence predicted both leadership practices and successful program implementation, with transformational leadership acting as a significant mediator between counselors' emotional competencies and program outcomes (Hilts et al., 2022).

Through coaching in emotional awareness, regulation, resilience, and conflict management, counselors help students develop positive coping mechanisms and adaptability. They also embody emotional competencies that enhance school-wide initiatives and foster supportive learning environments.

Early Intervention

Early intervention in social and emotional learning helps address challenges before they become persistent academic or behavioral difficulties. A comprehensive systematic review and meta-analysis of universal, curriculum-based SEL programs delivered in early childhood settings—spanning 79 studies and over 18,000 young children—demonstrated statistically significant improvements in social competence, emotional competence, behavioral self-regulation, early learning outcomes, and reductions in emotional and behavioral problems (Blewitt et al., 2018).

These results affirm that embedding SEL early supports foundational development across multiple domains, helping prevent later academic struggles or entrenched behavior issues.

The Head Start REDI intervention produced indirect benefits on high school emotional and behavioral outcomes through earlier improvements in social–emotional learning and family support, despite no direct effects on academic achievement (Bierman et al., 2025).

Integration of SEL in Curriculum

Integration of social-emotional learning into academic instruction ensures that emotional growth is valued alongside cognitive learning rather than treated as an optional supplement. A 2025 study in the *International Journal of Education and Pedagogy* outlined a structured framework for effective SEL integration. It identified four key dimensions—explicit skill instruction, embedded practice opportunities, teacher preparation, and ecological alignment—and argued that successful integration requires systematic curricular coordination supported by reliable assessment frameworks connecting SEL with academic outcomes (Premachandran, n.d.).

At the classroom level, interdisciplinary models show particular promise. For example, recent work published in *The Reading Teacher* demonstrated that literacy instruction can be enriched by embedding SEL competencies directly into early-grade reading practices. Through the use of contemporary picture books, educators paired SEL themes such as empathy, collaboration, and conflict resolution with literacy objectives, producing gains in both reading comprehension and social awareness (Deliman et al., 2024).

This evidence suggests that SEL integration need not compete with academic priorities but instead can amplify them, ensuring that students acquire essential emotional skills while advancing their literacy development.

Embedding SEL into academic lessons allows students to practice self-regulation, stress management, and interpersonal communication in authentic academic contexts. This approach strengthens engagement, nurtures reflective thinking, and reinforces academic achievement by linking emotional competencies with concrete learning experiences. By prioritizing SEL alongside traditional subjects, schools establish environments where both emotional and cognitive development are cultivated as interconnected elements of student success.

Socio-Economic and Environmental Influences

Persistent poverty, unstable home environments, and adverse community conditions exert a profound effect on students' academic achievement, particularly by disrupting cognitive and emotional development. An extensive longitudinal neuroimaging study of children and adolescents aged 4 to 22 years revealed that those from households below the federal poverty level had significantly reduced gray-matter volumes—3 to 4 percentage points lower among those below 150 percent of the poverty line and 8 to 10 points lower among those living below it—which mediated approximately 20 percent of the gap in standardized test scores between low-income and higher-income students (Hair et al., 2015).

These findings illustrate that socioeconomic disadvantage undermines academic potential not only through material scarcity but also via physiological pathways that impair brain development. Consequently, effective support systems must be equitable and responsive; they should include enhanced access to early enrichment, stable and nurturing home-school partnerships, and community resources to offset the developmental deficits associated with poverty.

Group Counseling and Peer Support

Group counseling and structured peer-support programs provide powerful avenues for enhancing students' social skills, self-esteem, and sense of belonging, with measurable benefits for emotional well-being and academic performance. A 2022 systematic review of 18 school-based group counseling interventions found that those incorporating informational content as a core therapeutic component achieved large effect sizes (above 0.8) for academic outcomes, underscoring the potential of well-designed peer group formats to support learning goals (Steen et al., 2022).

Furthermore, a meta-analysis conducted with Chinese mainland adolescents (involving 15,320 participants from 611 studies) documented that group counseling significantly improved learning motivation (SMD ≈ 0.95), academic self-efficacy (SMD ≈ 1.26), and learning engagement (SMD ≈ 1.48), while reducing negative behaviors such as procrastination and burnout (SMDs of about −1.53 and −1.59, respectively) (Lin et al., 2025).

These moderate-to-large standardized effects highlight group interventions as a particularly effective strategy for reinforcing emotional coping, peer connection, and academic resilience in school settings.

Trauma and Adverse Childhood Experiences (ACEs)

Given the profound effects of trauma on learning readiness, school counselors play a critical role in delivering trauma-informed care that acknowledges students' histories and responses as understandable adaptations rather than oppositional conduct. Counseling interventions that foster emotional safety, allow students to build trust, and offer adaptive coping strategies help mitigate trauma-related academic disruptions. Proper training in trauma-awareness equips counselors to shape supportive environments that restore students' capacity for engagement and self-regulation.

A 2019 article in *Professional School Counseling* outlines how trauma-sensitive school counseling programs, grounded in the Multi-Tiered System of Support (MTSS) framework, help create belonging, reduce retraumatization, and support academic engagement, especially for youth in foster care. The piece highlights that school counselors trained in trauma-informed practices can fundamentally enhance student access to learning, emotional safety, and academic success through integrated policy, practice, and collaboration (Martinez et al., 2020).

Collaboration and consistency among counselors, teachers, and parents are crucial in establishing a cohesive support system that fosters student growth. A collaborative model based on experiential learning—implemented among elementary school teachers, parents, and counselors—demonstrated notable reductions in non-academic behavioral issues, especially disrespectful and disruptive conduct. This model showed that joint engagement by parents and counselors substantially aids teachers in effectively addressing behavioral challenges (Darmiany et al., 2022).

Such collaboration enables alignment of goals, strategies, and messaging across the home and school settings. When counselors facilitate this collaboration, they help create an educational ecosystem characterized by mutual understanding, shared expectations, and consistent reinforcement of behavioral and academic strategies. This consistency reassures students, strengthens emotional security, and promotes coherent learning experiences. Therefore, joint efforts among all stakeholders not only enrich the school climate but also support sustained emotional and academic development.

Attendance, Engagement, and Dropout Prevention

Chronic absenteeism undermines both learning opportunities and overall student well-being, as students who are frequently absent tend to disengage academically and socially, thereby increasing their risk of dropping out. National data show that chronic absenteeism rose sharply post-pandemic—from about 15 percent in 2019 to nearly 30 percent by 2022—and although rates improved slightly to 27.9 percent in 2023, they remain far above pre-pandemic levels. Elevated absenteeism is strongly associated with lower graduation rates and reduced long-term success. For example, in one state, ninth graders who missed ten or more school days per year exhibited a graduation rate of only 41 percent or less, which underscores the urgency of addressing attendance as a core barrier to student success (Addis, 2024).

Social-emotional learning (SEL) plays a crucial role in enhancing attendance by improving school climate and promoting student engagement. When students feel emotionally safe, connected to teachers, and supported within the school community, they are more likely to attend consistently. SEL programs help create these conditions by nurturing caring relationships, promoting emotional regulation, and building resilience against stressors that commonly contribute to absenteeism (DESSA Team, 2023).

By addressing underlying social-emotional barriers to attendance, such as anxiety, disengagement, and isolation, school counselors help prevent dropout risks before they intensify. Interventions that focus on developing emotional self-awareness, building trusting relationships between adults and students, and facilitating peer support not only reduce absenteeism but also reinforce students' motivation, class participation, and academic persistence.

Long-Term Benefits of SEL Foundations

Foundational social-emotional skills extend well beyond immediate academic outcomes and contribute to long-term success in college, careers, relationships, and life satisfaction. A comprehensive review of hundreds of studies involving over one million PreK–12 students found that SEL programs produced lasting effects: students exposed to SEL achieved academic performance that was, on average, 11 percentile points higher, with benefits persisting years after program participation (up to 13 percentile points higher) (Collaborative for Academic, Social, and Emotional Learning, n.d.)

Beyond academic metrics, SEL fosters the core competencies required for effective personal and professional life—such as self-awareness, emotional regulation, empathy, responsible decision-making, and interpersonal collaboration. These abilities form the foundation of college and career readiness, enabling individuals to navigate complex social environments, communicate effectively, and manage stress and change.

Moreover, SEL contributes significantly to life satisfaction. Programs that build social-emotional skills promote healthier relationships, lower levels of anxiety and depression, and stronger coping mechanisms in the face of adversity. As a result, individuals who develop these competencies early tend to report better overall well-being, more meaningful connections, and greater resilience throughout their lives.

In summary, investing in SEL yields a dual return: it enhances academic outcomes while fostering the durable emotional and social capacities that underpin success in higher education, the workforce, and personal fulfillment.

Conclusion

The discussion in this chapter highlights the crucial role of social and emotional learning in promoting both academic achievement and comprehensive student development. The evidence reviewed across multiple domains demonstrates that emotional well-being forms a foundation upon which learning is built. Without emotional security and resilience, students face significant barriers to engagement, attendance, and achievement. Counselors are positioned as vital agents in this process, equipping students with the skills of self-regulation, empathy, adaptability, and conflict resolution while simultaneously guiding teachers and parents in creating consistent and supportive environments.

Equally important is the emphasis on early intervention and the integration of SEL within the curriculum. Addressing social and emotional needs at an early stage prevents the escalation of behavioral and academic difficulties, while embedding SEL in daily instruction ensures that emotional growth is not treated as secondary to cognitive development. When trauma, poverty, or unstable environments disrupt learning readiness, trauma-informed practices and equitable supports help restore the conditions necessary for success. These interventions are strengthened further through collaborative frameworks that unify the efforts of educators, families, and counselors.

Long-term outcomes reinforce the value of SEL, showing enduring benefits for college and career readiness, stronger interpersonal relationships, and overall life satisfaction. Research consistently points to higher academic performance, lower dropout rates, and improved well-being for students who have developed strong social and emotional foundations. Therefore, investment in

SEL is not a supplementary measure but a strategic approach that aligns educational systems with the broader goal of nurturing capable, resilient, and socially responsible individuals. By prioritizing SEL as an integral component of academic life, schools not only advance immediate learning outcomes but also contribute meaningfully to lifelong success.

⌒◯

Chapter 7:
The Impact of Technology

Technology's Dual Role in Counseling

Technology presents both advantages and challenges in student counseling. On the one hand, tools such as mobile well-being apps, mHealth platforms, SMS-based support, virtual messaging apps, online scheduling, and teletherapy enhance the accessibility and scalability of counseling services.

A systematic literature review of 19 studies (across countries such as Indonesia, the United States, Turkey, the Philippines, and Iran) found that these technological modalities consistently improved the reach and efficiency of educational counseling services (Muhammad, 2024).

These tools enable students residing in remote areas or those with mobility constraints to engage with counselors, reduce travel time, and sometimes increase the frequency of contact. Virtual platforms may also provide a sense of anonymity that lowers barriers related to stigma or discomfort.

On the other hand, these benefits come with significant challenges. Studies report issues such as loss of nonverbal cues (facial expression, tone), a weaker sense of rapport, and reduced mutual trust. Counselors may feel less effective when unable to perceive subtle emotional signals. Furthermore, privacy and confidentiality risks are absolute, especially in countries or institutions without robust data protection policies. Counselors often require additional training to use digital tools appropriately, and there is often resistance among both students and counselors to moving entirely online. A qualitative study of e-counseling in Jordan revealed that while teachers found digital counseling to be valuable and cost-effective, many noted that the lack of direct, face-to-face interaction weakened the effectiveness of the counseling process (Altarawneh, 2022).

Social Media and Mental Health

Social media platforms have a profound impact—both protective and harmful—on students' emotional well-being. Several recent empirical studies document correlations between problematic social media use and elevated levels of anxiety, depression, poorer sleep, and low self-esteem.

A cross-sectional study conducted in Lorestan province (Iran) during the COVID-19 pandemic surveyed 781 university students and measured problematic social media use via established scales (e.g., DASS-21 for depression/anxiety/stress). It found that problematic social media use had a strong positive association with worse mental health scores (higher anxiety, depression, stress). Factors such as household income, field of study, and marital status also played roles (Nazari et al., 2023).

Additional issues include cyberbullying, social comparison, fear of missing out (FOMO), and validation culture (seeking "likes" or followers), which can exacerbate distress when students perceive themselves as failing to meet idealized online standards. The passive consumption of perfected images or lifestyles can contribute to appearance anxiety and lower self-esteem.

Screen Time and Cognitive / Emotional Effects

Excessive screen time in students is increasingly linked to declines in attention, emotional regulation, and academic performance. A large-scale study using data from the China Education Panel Survey (CEPS) involving over 17,000 junior middle school students found significant negative correlations between screen time and performance in Chinese, mathematics, English, and composite academic scores. Most notably, screen use for gaming and general internet usage had the most substantial adverse effects.

Path analyses in that same study revealed that cognitive performance serves as the principal mediator of the relationship between screen time and academic performance, with sleep duration, mental health, classmate relationships, and parent-child relationships acting as secondary mediators (Feng, Ren, and Shi, 2025).

Emotional regulation is also compromised by excessive screen exposure. A recent cross-sectional study among university students in Thailand (n = 446) measured excessive digital screen time (EDST) and found strong associations with poor mental health (higher scores for anxiety and depression), worse sleep quality, low self-esteem, loneliness, and lower academic performance. Younger students and those in demanding programs (such as health sciences) were more affected (Feng et al., 2025).

Attention span difficulties are often reported. In the CEPS-based study, students with high levels of screen exposure (especially when using devices for social media or gaming) showed more difficulty sustaining attention, slower information processing, and lower retention in class. Experts note that multitasking with screens (e.g., switching between social media, messaging, games, and homework) compounds these effects.

Together, these findings suggest that screen time is not uniformly negative, but that *type*, *duration*, and *context* matter. Passive screen use (e.g., long videos, social media scrolling) and use late in the day negatively affect sleep, which further worsens emotional regulation, increases anxiety, and reduces academic achievement.

Digital Citizenship and Responsible Use

Digital citizenship encompasses the knowledge, skills, attitudes, and behaviors that enable students to engage online safely, ethically, and productively. Counselors play a key role in guiding students toward responsible use of technology, promoting online safety, and striking a balance between online and offline life.

The ASCA Position Statement (2023) defines that school counselors have the responsibility to educate students and families about responsible use of interactive digital technologies, digital citizenship, cultural, ethical, and legal considerations. Counselors collaborate with families, educators, and other stakeholders to promote safe content, digital footprint awareness, and cyber-balance (American School Counselor Association, n.d.).

Evidence is accumulating that structured digital citizenship education programs also have measurable outcomes. In a cluster randomized controlled trial of the *Be Internet Awesome* curriculum, involving 1,072 grades 4-6 students across 14 schools, the program significantly improved students' knowledge, attitudes, and behaviors related to online safety, privacy, respectful interaction, and digital responsibility (Jones et al., 2023).

Media literacy is an essential component of responsible use. Through media literacy, students learn to critically evaluate sources, identify misinformation, understand the dynamics of algorithms and platforms, and reflect on how online content influences their beliefs, self-image, and behavior. Counselors can integrate media literacy lessons into counseling sessions or collaborate with teachers to embed them in curricula.

In addition, counselors can support students in balancing online and offline life by:

- Encouraging scheduled tech-free times (especially before sleep),

- Promoting physical activities and face-to-face social interactions,

- Advising on privacy settings, appropriate content, and respectful online communication,

- Helping students develop self-regulation skills around device use.

Interventions and Coping Strategies

Counseling for problematic social media use should combine evidence-based psychotherapy with practical behaviour change techniques. Cognitive behavioural therapy (CBT) and CBT-informed brief interventions target maladaptive thoughts that drive compulsive checking, and teach concrete skills such as stimulus control, activity scheduling, and graded exposure to reduce use. Clinical reviews indicate that therapy-based interventions produce larger improvements in mood and addiction symptoms than simple restriction or abstinence programs (Plackett et al., 2023).

Group formats and web-delivered brief programmes can increase access and reduce cost without sacrificing core therapeutic elements. Trials summarized in recent reviews demonstrate that structured web group sessions enhance self-regulation and mitigate internet-use problems when they incorporate goal setting, monitoring, and relapse prevention components. Where severe addictive patterns exist or comorbid psychiatric symptoms are present, multi-modal approaches that combine psychotherapy with specialist medical input have shown more potent effects in randomized trials. For internet-use disorders, the highest-quality evidence, summarized in a network meta-analysis, identified combinations such as CBT with adjunctive biological or neuromodulation approaches as among the more efficacious interventions, although heterogeneity between trials remains substantial (Zhu et al., 2023).

Parental and Community Involvement

Parents and caregivers are central agents of change for children's digital habits. Interventions that involve caregivers—through education, modelling, and home rules—produce measurable reductions in children's screen time and improvements in family routines. Randomized and quasi-experimental studies indicate that parent-focused education and coaching, which set clear limits, model balanced use, and increase parental self-efficacy, yield meaningful declines in daily screen exposure among young children. These programs are most effective when combined with school support and consistent messaging across home and school settings (Kaur et al., 2024).

Schools and community organizations should adopt coordinated strategies that align policy, curriculum, and family outreach. Counselors can facilitate this alignment by providing brief trainings for parents on practical steps (consistent bedtimes, device-free family meals, use of parental controls), by hosting workshops that model media-use conversations, and by developing simple take-home agreements that families can adapt. Community engagement also includes linking families to local resources for mental health, physical activity opportunities, and tutoring, which together replace passive screen time with structured, socially engaging alternatives.

Finally, evaluation and iterative improvement are essential. Programs should track simple outcomes, such as average daily screen time, sleep quality, and classroom attention, and use these metrics to refine their approaches. Evidence to date supports multi-component, family-centered interventions as the most reliable path to sustained behavior change and improved emotional and academic outcomes (Zhu et al., 2023).

Emerging Digital Mental Health Supports

Digital mental health interventions (DMHIs) are increasingly integrated into school counselling as supplemental tools that extend access, flexibility, and monitoring capacity while preserving the central role of human counsellors. Recent systematic reviews indicate that interventions such as internet-delivered cognitive behavioral therapy (iCBT), app-based self-help programs, and brief guided modules produce small to moderate reductions in anxiety and depressive symptoms among children and adolescents, and that effects are larger when human support or therapist guidance is included. These interventions also enhance reach by reducing geographic and scheduling barriers, which is particularly important for under-resourced or remote communities (Fernández-Batanero et al., 2025).

Counsellors can safely leverage DMHIs in three complementary ways: first, as low-threshold entry points that help students recognize symptoms and access brief self-help while waiting for in-person services; second, as adjuncts that reinforce in-session learning through homework, monitoring, and skills practice; and third, as population-level screening and monitoring tools that flag students at risk for targeted follow-up. Programs that combine automated content with periodic clinician check-ins demonstrate better adherence and lower dropout rates than fully unguided tools, making them more suitable for school settings where continuity and engagement are crucial (Fernández-Batanero et al., 2025).

Quality assurance and risk management are essential. Not all digital tools are evidence-based, and some lack adequate safety provisions for managing acute risk or suicidality. Counselors should prioritize products that have published efficacy data, clear privacy policies, clinical oversight, and established crisis pathways. Where possible, schools should adopt formal procurement standards that require third-party evaluations, data security compliance, and procedures for integrating digital outputs into existing referral pathways. Training counsellors on digital triage, app metric interpretation, and ethical data use is necessary to ensure that technology enhances rather than fragments care.

Policy and professional guidance increasingly emphasize the role of schools in shaping healthier online environments. Global health authorities emphasize that digital support must be part of a comprehensive strategy that includes promoting offline social support, sleep hygiene, and the design of safe platforms. Schools and counsellors have a responsibility to help students use digital resources wisely, to teach digital literacy about how to evaluate online mental health information, and to ensure that digital options do not replace timely, face-to-face clinical care when needed. Adoption of DMHIs should therefore be strategic, supervised, and outcome-driven (World Health Organization, 2024).

Counselors occupy a central position in guiding students toward healthy, balanced, and purposeful engagement with digital technologies. Their role is not to discourage technology use, but to ensure that digital tools function as supports for learning, connection, and well-being rather than as sources of harm. This bridging role requires both technical awareness and sensitivity to the social and emotional needs of students.

Counselors as Bridges Between Technology and Well-Being

Research indicates that when technology is integrated with appropriate oversight, it can enhance academic achievement, expand access to support services, and foster stronger peer collaboration. At the same time, uncontrolled or excessive use of digital platforms is linked with distraction, poor sleep, diminished social interaction, and increased anxiety. Counselors, therefore, help students and families navigate this dual reality by providing guidance, structured interventions, and ongoing monitoring.

As professionals, counselors are positioned to evaluate which tools are evidence-based, age-appropriate, and aligned with developmental goals. They can introduce students to digital mental health supports or educational applications while reinforcing critical skills such as self-regulation, media literacy, and digital citizenship. In addition, counselors play an advocacy role by collaborating with teachers, administrators, and parents to develop policies that promote balance, protect privacy, and foster respectful online behavior.

The ultimate goal is to transform technology into an ally of growth. When used thoughtfully, digital tools can provide opportunities for self-expression, peer support, and accessible mental health care. Counselors ensure that these opportunities are connected to offline practices that build resilience, interpersonal skills, and academic motivation. By acting as mediators between technology and student development, counselors help shape an environment where digital engagement strengthens rather than undermines well-being.

In conclusion, the counselor's role is to balance innovation with responsibility. By guiding students, families, and schools in the mindful use of digital tools, counselors ensure that technology supports the academic, social, and emotional flourishing of young people.

Chapter 8:
School Counselors as Agents of Change

School counselors must move beyond offering support only to individual students and assume roles as advocates for systemic change in education. This shift entails influencing policies, procedures, and school culture to ensure that social and emotional well-being is given equal weight alongside academic achievement. When counselors are seen as leaders in school improvement, they help schools adopt holistic, student-centered approaches. Such approaches integrate social-emotional learning, mental health supports, and equity considerations into everyday school practice, rather than treating them as add-ons.

To effect systemic change, counselors need robust evidence of their program's effectiveness. Data-driven strategies allow them to demonstrate outcomes, set goals, measure progress, and communicate results to stakeholders. For example, recent research has shown that when school counselling programs collect and analyze student data on attendance, behavior, academic performance, and emotional health, those programs gain greater support from administrators and policymakers. One study of state-level departments of education in the United States found that evaluation tools developed for school counselling not only helped identify gaps in service delivery but also improved accountability, leading to increased resource allocations in many districts (Geesa et al., 2024).

Another recent study titled "The Use of Implementation Strategies in School Counseling" explored how school counselors involved in Recognized ASCA Model Programs (RAMP) used data for planning, monitoring, and refinement of program components. The study demonstrated that data use enhanced program fidelity, fostered stakeholder buy-in, and helped justify additional staffing or funding when trends in student outcome metrics were shared with school leadership (Warren et al., 2025).

Counselors seeking to advocate successfully should follow several key steps: first, collect disaggregated data across student groups (by income, race, gender, etc.) to uncover inequities; second, align counseling goals with school improvement plans so that outcomes are relevant to decision-makers; third, communicate results through reports, meetings, and dashboards to make impact visible; and fourth, use data to argue for more or better resources, such as lower student-to-counselor ratios, full-time counsellors, or expanded mental health services.

When school counselors utilize data in a structured manner, they gain credibility and authority to advocate for systemic reforms, ensuring that support services are not optional extras but are integral to school success. Counselors thus become bridges between individual student needs and broader educational policy, creating environments where well-being and academic success mutually reinforce each other.

Partnering with Policymakers for Policy Reform

School counselors must actively engage with policy to ensure that all students receive fair access to mental health supports and counseling. This includes working with policymakers to reform policies that currently limit access for some students, promoting equity and inclusion, and advocating for modern, comprehensive school mental health programs.

Counselors can form alliances with school boards, district officials, state education agencies, and legislators to review existing policies that create barriers to counseling. For example, restrictive funding models, staffing ratios, and eligibility criteria for services often exclude marginalized students. In many jurisdictions, the number of counselors per student remains far above recommended standards, disadvantaging schools with low-income, rural, or minority populations. By presenting evidence of disparities in access, counselors can prompt policy changes such as mandated counselor staffing levels, reforms to attendance and disciplinary policies that reduce exclusion, and laws that support universal school mental health services.

Addressing Disparities through Diversity, Equity, and Inclusion (DEI)

A recent study, "An Exploration of the Impact of the School Counseling Equity Landscape" (2025), examined how systemic discrimination persists despite greater demographic diversity in U.S. schools. The authors found that students from marginalized racial or socioeconomic groups often receive less access to comprehensive counseling services, a lower likelihood of referrals for advanced mental health support, and weaker outcomes when services are available. Counselors must utilize DEI frameworks to identify these gaps in their districts, advocate for culturally responsive practices, and ensure that resources are allocated in a way that serves all groups equitably (Merlin-Knoblich et al., 2025).

Another study, "Disparities in Access to Mental Health Services Among Children" (2023), documented that children in under-resourced communities confronted multiple structural barriers— including fewer school-based mental health staff, longer wait times, and less telehealth availability—that reduced service receipt. This study recommends policy interventions, including funding shifts, legislation to mandate services in underserved districts, and incentives for mental health practitioners to work in high-need schools (Mahmood et al., 2024).

Challenging Outdated Policies and Advocating Comprehensiveness

Outdated policies often assume mental health supports as optional extras rather than essential components of the educational mission. Counselors should advocate for policy revisions that mandate comprehensive mental health programming in schools. Comprehensive programs include prevention, early intervention, counseling, crisis services, family engagement, and after-school supports. Such programs require stable funding, clear accountability, and integration into school improvement plans.

In sum, policy and equity work is not peripheral to school counseling; it is central. Counselors who effectively partner with policymakers, use data to reveal disparities, integrate DEI principles, and push for policy modernization can help transform school systems. Their advocacy ensures that mental health support becomes universally accessible, allowing every student, regardless of background, to thrive academically, socially, and emotionally.

Working with External Partners to Expand Resources

School counselors who form partnerships with community health agencies, non-profits, and private sector providers often gain access to additional resources such as funding, specialized staff, training, and referral networks. For example, a 2024 study of school-based mental health services in the U.S. found that partnerships with external providers were increasingly used to close gaps in service delivery. These partnerships enabled schools to offer group interventions, telehealth support, and family counseling that would not have been available otherwise (Panchal, Cox, & Rudowitz, 2025).

An illustrative case is a grant awarded to George Mason University and its partners to serve Manassas City Public Schools. The grant, with nearly US$5 million over five years, is being used to train mental health service providers within high-need K-12 public schools. It includes collaboration between the university, college partners, and the local district. This partnership increases both workforce capacity and service quality (Panchal, Cox, & Rudowitz, 2025).

Strengthening Systemic Impact Through Partnerships

For systemic impact, collaboration must be intentional and embedded in practice. First, counselors should map local community assets by identifying agencies, programs, and private organizations that can support interventions. Asset mapping helps reveal untapped partners, such as mental health clinics, local charities, or civic organizations. This approach has been demonstrated in qualitative studies to enhance a school's ability to offer comprehensive support to students and their families (Dogan, Dollarhide, & Julian, 2021).

Second, formal agreements (such as Memoranda of Understanding) can set clear roles, expectations, and accountability. These agreements help avoid duplication, permit shared funding, and streamline referral systems across agencies. Additionally, local governments can offer policy support and funding incentives. For example, grants from state or federal sources can be contingent on collaborative plans. This encourages schools to build partnerships proactively, not just opportunistically.

Finally, private institutions such as universities or nonprofit foundations often bring expertise in program evaluation, staff training, or research capacity. These partnerships enable school counselors to assess outcomes, refine program design, and develop scalable models.

Leveraging Networks and Associations

Engagement with professional organizations gives school counselors forums to share best practices, learn from peers, and coordinate collective action. For example, the American School Counselor Association (ASCA) maintains the National Model, which outlines professional standards and ethical competencies, providing a common language for advocacy and practice. These resources help counselors align their work with recognized benchmarks (American School Counselor Association, n.d.)

Committing to Continuous Professional Development

To stay current, counselors must commit to continual learning. This includes reading recent research, attending workshops, engaging in online and in-person training, and participating in communities of practice. For instance, trauma-informed care is emerging as a key area: a recent professional development program for counselors and teachers improved compassion satisfaction (workers' sense of meaning and capability) and reduced secondary traumatic stress. These changes enabled practitioners to provide better emotional and psychological support to students (Perryman et al., 2025).

Continuous professional development also builds the skills necessary to interpret data, integrate technology, and design inclusive programs. When counselors bring up-to-date evidence into meetings with stakeholders, their arguments gain weight. When they understand new digital tools, cultural trends, or policy shifts, they can adapt quickly and propose innovations that respond to current student needs.

Through professional affiliation and personal investment in learning, school counselors amplify their voice. In unified networks, they can influence legislation, funding decisions, and school policies. Individually, they become more effective in their roles, bringing clarity, insight, and authority to their work. Together, these efforts help ensure that the school counseling profession is not only responsive but also proactive, capable of shaping the future of education in equitable, evidence-based ways.

Counselors as Change Agents

School counselors today are called to balance the immediate guidance they provide to individual students with broader efforts that promote long-term educational reform. While one-on-one counseling remains central to the profession, it is increasingly evident that systemic challenges like inequitable access to mental health resources, outdated policies, and persistent disparities cannot be addressed through individual work alone. Counselors who step into the role of change agents bridge this gap by combining daily practice with advocacy for reform at the school, district, and policy levels.

As practitioners, counselors help students manage academic, emotional, and social needs. As leaders, they analyze data, identify inequities, and push for reforms that create healthier and more supportive learning environments. By engaging with administrators, policymakers, and community stakeholders, counselors ensure that their insights from direct student work inform systemic decision-making. This dual role strengthens the profession's impact, moving beyond isolated interventions to structural improvements that benefit entire student populations.

Counselors who embrace this responsibility are also leaders in shaping school culture. They encourage a shift toward holistic, student-centered approaches where emotional well-being and inclusion are viewed as essential to academic success. Through collaboration with teachers, families, and external partners, counselors help schools implement comprehensive programs that integrate prevention, early intervention, and support services.

Ultimately, the counselor's role as a change agent lies in fostering both personal growth for students and institutional transformation for schools. When counselors advocate for equity, model best practices, and pursue ongoing professional growth, they create conditions in which meaningful reform is not only possible but sustainable. This dual focus ensures that students are supported in the present while systems are restructured to provide fair, effective, and lasting support for future generations.

$\smile\hspace{-0.3em}\multimap$

Chapter 9:
The Future of School Counseling and Lasting Impact

School counseling has undergone a significant transformation, shifting from individual guidance and crisis management to a comprehensive role integrated within the education system. This text has explored the intricate duties of the contemporary school counselor, whose influence extends across the entire student journey and school culture. The role requires a sophisticated equilibrium: offering direct, personalized assistance for academic, emotional, and social difficulties while also addressing systemic obstacles that hinder wider student achievement. This dual approach means counselors address both immediate concerns and their underlying causes, establishing a sustainable framework that supports both present and future students.

The growing emphasis on mental health in education has further established the school counselor as a vital component in student development. Amid the pervasive impact of social media, heightened academic demands, and evolving societal standards, counselors are primary guardians of student wellness. Their responsibilities now include directly teaching crucial life abilities—such as managing emotions, practicing digital citizenship, building resilience, and handling stress—skills now considered as important for lifelong success as academic learning. This broader mission demands strong, ongoing collaboration. School counselors must create and maintain integrated support networks that unite teachers, administrators, families, and community resources. The success of these initiatives increasingly relies on data-driven methods; by demonstrating their effect on attendance, grades, and behavior, counselors can powerfully argue for the necessary resources, staff, and institutional reforms.

The Future of School Counseling

The profession's path forward will be molded by powerful, converging trends reshaping education. Rising mental health requirements, significant policy discussions, and the dual nature of technological progress place unprecedented pressure on schools, with counselors at the heart of these changes. The field is advancing toward a future where its worth and effectiveness will be judged by its power to shape school-wide policy and climate, demanding a practice that reaches well outside the counseling office. Successful counselors will be those who adopt roles as systemic reformers, leaders in social-emotional curriculum, and designers of equitable, nurturing school settings for all learners.

Mental Health Awareness and Student Needs

A significant cultural shift over the last decade has solidified the understanding that student mental health is closely tied to educational success. Issues like anxiety, depression, and persistent stress are now acknowledged as frequent challenges that directly affect a student's ability to learn, build healthy connections, and develop self-worth. For school counseling, this requires moving past a mainly reactive support model. Future practice will position counselors as mental health leaders in their schools, advocating for a community-wide focus on psychological wellness. This includes implementing trauma-informed methods that change how all staff engage with students, creating school-wide resilience and mental health education programs, and working to reduce the stigma of seeking support. The counselor's office transforms into the central point for a culture that actively values mental well-being.

Policy Shifts and Equity

The reach, caliber, and sustainability of robust school counseling programs are deeply influenced by legislative and regulatory decisions at all levels of government. Passive acceptance of policy is unsustainable for a profession committed to respect for all. The future requires school counselors to actively participate in policy formation, turning their direct experience into persuasive arguments. They offer a vital, human perspective on data, showing how unfair funding, insufficient staff numbers, and limiting legislation create obstacles for marginalized students—including those from low-income households, students of color, and rural populations.

This forward-thinking involvement in policy is the most straightforward path to establishing school counseling not as an optional extra, but as a core element of a sound education. The objective is to cement into policy the essentials for success, including enforced lower student-to-counselor ratios, dedicated funding, and assurances of fair services in all districts.

Technology and New Tools

The digital age presents a lasting dilemma for the field. While technology—especially smartphones and social media—is a proven source of increased anxiety, social comparison, and distraction for young people, it also provides innovative support mechanisms. The thoughtful and ethical adoption of these digital resources will characterize counseling's future. Teletherapy and online communication are overcoming geographical and stigma-related barriers, offering critical access for students in isolated areas or those hesitant to meet in person.

Numerous applications of mindfulness, mood monitoring, and cognitive behavioral techniques provide students with methods for self-management. School counselors will increasingly act as curators of these digital tools, advising on their proper application and ensuring technology enhances, rather than replaces, the crucial therapeutic relationship. At the same time, counselors must integrate digital citizenship and media literacy into their teaching, helping students navigate the online world with safety, critical thinking, and responsibility.

Staffing Ratios and Professional Support

The gap between ideal and real student-to-counselor ratios remains a primary barrier to effective practice. Caseloads in the hundreds, still typical in many places, make a thorough, developmental counseling program unfeasible, often reducing professionals to constant crisis management. The profession's long-term health and success depend on a determined, multi-tiered effort to address this fundamental issue.

This involves showing decision-makers clear evidence connecting proper ratios to better student results, from increased graduation rates to enhanced school climate. Alongside campaigning for more staff, the field must develop strong, multi-level professional support systems for counselors. The emotional weight of the job is substantial, and without intentional frameworks for mentorship, professional learning groups, and peer support, the danger of burnout and turnover is significant. Supporting counselor well-being and ongoing development is a strategic imperative, not a mere administrative perk, for preserving an expert and dedicated workforce.

Leadership and Professional Development

The growing complexity of education necessitates that school counselors assume leadership roles, regardless of their official title. Here, leadership is about influence and vision—the capacity to affect school-wide goals and ensure choices in classrooms, administrative offices, and government are guided by a complete understanding of the child. Counselors have a distinct, system-wide perspective, interacting with students, parents, teachers, and leaders across all areas. This vantage point makes them strong proponents of policies and practices that aid student wellness, whether reforming disciplinary systems to be more restorative, advocating for later school start times aligned with sleep science, or ensuring that new academic programs include suitable social-emotional components. This leadership role is tied to a dedication to continuous learning. Knowledge in neuroscience, trauma, technology, and culturally responsive methods is always advancing. Counselors must therefore be lifelong learners, pursuing ongoing development through advanced courses, conferences, professional organizations, and independent study to keep their practices grounded in evidence, current, and aligned with the needs of their students.

Collaboration and Innovation

No one person or office can meet the diverse needs of an entire student population. Thus, the future of effective school counseling is inherently cooperative. Counselors must act as the hub of an extensive support network, deliberately forming and sustaining strategic alliances with classroom teachers, school leaders, family members, community mental health organizations, and local partners. This collaborative safety net ensures students receive consistent, reinforced support, with the counselor often serving as a key communicator and coordinator among these different groups.

Alongside cooperation, an innovative mindset is necessary for future challenges. This extends beyond technology to encompass innovative service methods. Counselors will need to develop and apply new strategies such as multi-tiered support systems that distribute resources effectively, group sessions that foster community and address shared issues, peer mentoring initiatives that utilize student leadership, and culturally relevant practices that connect with diverse groups. This readiness to create and adjust is vital for reaching all students, especially those who have been traditionally left behind.

Call to Action

The future described here—where every student benefits from a thorough, fair, and impactful school counseling program—will not happen by chance. It demands a persistent, united, and strategic advocacy effort from counselors, their professional groups, and allies. This work must look inward, within school walls, to gain administrative backing and define the counselor's function, and outward, toward school boards, state governments, and the public, to secure essential funding and policy reforms.

The fundamental message is that school counselors are not an optional extra but are vital for achieving education's core mission: preparing every student for success in higher education, the workforce, and civic life. The task is challenging, requiring a unique blend of compassion, analytical ability, political acumen, and perseverance. Its effect, however, is profound, influencing individual lives and helping build a more empathetic, fair, and healthy society. The demand for skilled, dedicated school counselors is immense, and their pivotal role in creating schools where all students can thrive will only continue to grow in significance.

Bibliography

1. ACT, Inc. (n.d.). *College readiness begins in middle school* [Policy report]. https://files.eric.ed.gov/fulltext/ED483849.pdf

2. Addis, S. (2024). *A solution for the post-pandemic student attendance crisis* [White paper]. National Dropout Prevention Center & Successful Practices Network. Retrieved from https://dropoutprevention.org/wp-content/uploads/2024/03/Whitepaper_A-Solution-to-the-Attendance-Crisis.pdf

3. Alexander, E. R., Savitz-Romer, M., Nicola, T. P., & Carroll, S. (2022). "We are the heartbeat of the school": How school counselors supported student mental health during the COVID-19 pandemic. *Professional School Counseling, 26*(1), 1–12. https://doi.org/10.1177/2156759X221111007

4. Al-Jbouri, E., Andrews, N. C. Z., Peddigrew, E., Fortier, A., & Weaver, T. (2023). Building elementary students' social and emotional skills: A randomized control trial to evaluate a teacher-led intervention. *School Mental Health, 15*(1), 138–150. https://doi.org/10.1007/s12310-022-09538-x

5. Altarawneh, A. M. A. (2022). The reality of E-counseling services in the light of digital learning from the perspective of teachers in Jordan. *Education and Information Technologies, 27*(7), 9311-9328. https://doi.org/10.1007/s10639-022-11215-5

6. American School Counselor Association. (n.d.). Events & professional development. ASCA. Retrieved July 14, 2025,

from https://www.schoolcounselor.org/Events-Professional-Development/Professional-Development

7. American School Counselor Association. (2021). The school counselor and school counselor supervision [Position statement]. ASCA. https://www.schoolcounselor.org/Standards-Positions/Position-Statements/ASCA-Position-Statements/The-School-Counselor-and-School-Counselor-Supervis

8. American School Counselor Association. (2023). *2023 RAMP stories: Closing the gap* [PDF]. American School Counselor Association. https://www.schoolcounselor.org/getmedia/16a9b7f7-6a1b-4d93-abb9-4388aada343a/2023-RAMP-Stories.pdf

9. Bardhoshi, G., Schweinle, A., & Duncan, K. (2014). Understanding the impact of school factors on school counselor burnout: A mixed-methods study. *The Professional Counselor, 4*(5), 426–443. https://files.eric.ed.gov/fulltext/EJ1063202.pdf

10. Bardhoshi, G., Schweinle, A., & Duncan, K. (2025). Understanding the impact of school factors on school counselor burnout: A mixed-methods study. *The Professional Counselor, 15*(5). https://tpcjournal.nbcc.org/understanding-the-impact-of-school-factors-on-school-counselor-burnout-a-mixed-methods-study/

11. Bierman, K. L., Heinrichs, B. S., Welsh, J. A., Jones, D. E., & Crowley, D. M. (2025). How a preschool intervention affected high school outcomes: Longitudinal pathways in a randomized-

controlled trial. *Child Development, 96*(3), 1236–1249.
https://doi.org/10.1111/cdev.14235

12. Blake, M. K. (2020). Other duties as assigned: The ambiguous role of the high school counselor. *Sociology of Education, 93*(4), 315–330. https://doi.org/10.1177/0038040720932563

13. Blewitt, C., Fuller-Tyszkiewicz, M., Nolan, A., Bergmeier, H., Vicary, D., Huang, T., McCabe, P., McKay, T., & Skouteris, H. (2018). Social and emotional learning associated with universal curriculum-based interventions in early childhood education and care centers: A systematic review and meta-analysis. *JAMA Network Open, 1*(8), e185727.
https://doi.org/10.1001/jamanetworkopen.2018.5727

14. Brown, C. H., & Knight, D. (2023). Staffing schools to support the classroom: Examining student-to-school-counselor ratios and academic student outcomes in Texas. *Professional School Counseling, 27*(1).
https://doi.org/10.1177/2156759X231165497

15. Brown, C. H., & Knight, D. (2024). Student-to-school counselor ratios: Understanding the history and ethics behind professional staffing recommendations and realities in the United States (EdWorkingPaper No. 24-977). Annenberg Institute at Brown University. https://doi.org/10.26300/pzh5-6t96

16. Catapult Learning. (2025, February 10). Catapult Learning survey of K-12 school counselors reveals critical shortfalls in addressing youth mental health crisis [News release]. FullBloom. https://fullbloom.org/news/catapult-learning-

survey-of-k-12-school-counselors-reveals-critical-shortfalls-in-addressing-youth-mental-health-crisis/

17. Catapult Learning. (2025, March 3). School counselors ID "critical shortfalls" in student mental health crisis. *eSchool News*. Retrieved from https://www.eschoolnews.com/sel/2025/03/03/school-counselors-shortfalls-student-mental-health-crisis

18. Chu, T., Liu, X., Takayanagi, S., Matsushita, T., & Kishimoto, H. (2023). Association between mental health and academic performance among university undergraduates: The interacting role of lifestyle behaviors. *International Journal of Methods in Psychiatric Research, 32*(1), e1938. https://doi.org/10.1002/mpr.1938

19. Cipriano, C., Strambler, M. J., Naples, L. H., Ha, C., Kirk, M., Wood, M., Sehgal, K., Zieher, A. K., Eveleigh, A., McCarthy, M., Funaro, M., Ponnock, A., Chow, J. C., & Durlak, J. (2023). The state of evidence for social and emotional learning: A contemporary meta-analysis of universal school-based SEL interventions. *Child Development, 94*(5), 1181–1204. https://doi.org/10.1111/cdev.13968

20. Clemens, E. V., Carey, J. C., & Harrington, K. M. (2010). The School Counseling Program Implementation Survey: Initial instrument development and exploratory factor analysis. *Professional School Counseling, 14*(2), 125–134. https://doi.org/10.5330/prsc.14.2.k811174041n40l11

21. Collaborative for Academic, Social, and Emotional Learning. (n.d.). What does the research say? In *Fundamentals of SEL*.

Retrieved July 14, 2025, from https://casel.org/fundamentals-of-sel/what-does-the-research-say/

22. Collins, G., Kovac, K., Rigney, G., Benveniste, T., Gerace, A., Dittman, C. K., & Vincent, G. E. (2024). Parental expectations of school counsellors and their role in supporting student mental health and wellbeing: A qualitative study. *Journal of Psychologists and Counsellors in Schools, 34*(4), 415–432. https://doi.org/10.1177/20556365241298071

23. Dahir, C. A., & Stone, C. B. (2009). School counselor accountability: The path to social justice and systemic change. *Journal of Counseling & Development, 87*(Winter), 12–20. https://eric.ed.gov/?id=EJ826751

24. Darmiany, D., Gunayasa, I. B. K., Asrin, A., & Maulyda, M. A. (2022). Collaboration of teachers, parents, and counselors in overcoming non-academic problems of elementary school students. *Jurnal Ilmiah Sekolah Dasar, 6*(2), 306–318. https://doi.org/10.23887/jisd.v6i2.44332

25. Davis, L., Harward, K., & Yazzie, A. (2024). Parental expectations of school counsellors and their role in supporting student mental health and wellbeing: A qualitative study. *Professional School Counseling*. Advance online publication. https://doi.org/10.1177/20556365241298071

26. Deliman, A., Robertson, M. K., & Turner, R. K. (2024). Combining social-emotional learning competencies and contemporary concerns picturebooks to foster early literacy practices: An interdisciplinary approach. *The Reading Teacher, 78*(3), 165–176. https://doi.org/10.1002/trtr.2357

27. DESSA Team. (2023, September 12). Reduce chronic absenteeism with SEL. Aperture Education. Retrieved from https://apertureed.com/blog/reduce-chronic-absenteeism-social-emotional-learning/

28. Dogan, S., Dollarhide, C. T., & Julian, D. (2021). School counselors and school-community partnerships: Perceptions from school counselors. *Journal of School Counseling, 19*(5). https://jsc.montana.edu/articles/v19n5.pdf

29. Duncan, K., Brown-Rice, K., & Bardhoshi, G. (2014). Perceptions of the importance and utilization of clinical supervision among certified rural school counselors. *Professional School Counseling, 4*(5), 444–454. https://eric.ed.gov/?id=EJ1063211

30. Feng, X., Ren, S., & Shi, P. (2025). The relationship and mechanism of screen time and academic performance among adolescents: An empirical study based on CEPS. *Frontiers in Public Health, 13*. https://doi.org/10.3389/fpubh.2025.1533327

31. Fernández-Batanero, J. M., Fernández-Cerero, J., Montenegro-Rueda, M., & Fernández-Cerero, D. (2025). Effectiveness of digital mental health interventions for children and adolescents. *Children, 12*(3), Article 353. https://doi.org/10.3390/children12030353

32. Frank, A., DeDiego, A. C., Farrell, I. C., Jones, K., & Tracy, A. C. (2025). School counseling roles across states: A content analysis using the ASCA National Model. *The Professional Counselor, 15*(2), 148–163. https://doi.org/10.15241/af.15.2.148

33. Geesa, R. L., Elam, N. P., Quick, M. M., Odell, K. M., & Kim, J. (2024). Leading and supporting school counselors through evaluation systems: A national study. *Psychology in the Schools, 61*(3), 1090-1115. https://doi.org/10.1002/pits.23102

34. George Mason University. (2025, June 4). George Mason awarded $5 million from U.S. Department of Education to increase school counselors in high-need schools. George Mason University. Retrieved from https://www.gmu.edu/news/2025-06/george-mason-awarded-5-million-us-department-education-increase-school-counselors-high

35. Goodman-Scott, E., Betters-Bubon, J., & Donohue, P. (2015). Aligning comprehensive school counseling programs and positive behavioral interventions and supports to maximize school counselors' efforts. *Professional School Counseling, 19*(1), 57–67. https://doi.org/10.5330/1096-2409-19.1.57

36. Goodman-Scott, E., Sink, C. A., Cholewa, B. E., & Burgess, M. (2018). An ecological view of school counselor ratios and student academic outcomes: A national investigation. *Journal of Counseling & Development, 96*(4), 388–398. https://doi.org/10.1002/jcad.12221

37. Gordillo, W., & Haring, J. (2025). *Prioritizing student wellness through the whole child approach* [White paper]. Public Consulting Group. https://publicconsultinggroup.com/wp-content/uploads/2025/04/Whole-Child-Approach_Student-Wellness_White-Paper.pdf

38. Hair, N. L., Hanson, J. L., Wolfe, B. L., & Pollak, S. D. (2015). Association of child poverty, brain development, and academic

achievement. *JAMA Pediatrics, 169*(9), 822–829. https://doi.org/10.1001/jamapediatrics.2015.1475

39. Hannor-Walker, T., Pincus, R., Wright, L. S., Rock, W., Money-Brady, J., & Bohecker, L. (2022). School counselors and administrators agree: Time and testing are barriers. *International Journal of Education Policy and Leadership, 18*(2). https://doi.org/10.22230/ijepl.2021v18n2a1423

40. Hatch, T., & Chen-Hayes, S. F. (2008). School counselor beliefs about ASCA National Model school counseling program components using the SCPCS. *Professional School Counseling, 12*(1), 34–42. https://doi.org/10.1177/2156759X0801200104

41. Hilts, D., Liu, Y., & Luke, M. (2022). School counselors' emotional intelligence and comprehensive school counseling program implementation: The mediating role of transformational leadership. *The Professional Counselor, 12*(3), 232–248. https://doi.org/10.15241/dh.12.3.232

42. Jones, L. M., Mitchell, K. J., & Beseler, C. L. (2023). The impact of youth digital citizenship education: Insights from a cluster randomized controlled trial outcome evaluation of the Be Internet Awesome (BIA) curriculum. *Contemporary School Psychology, 28*(3), 509-523. https://doi.org/10.1007/s40688-023-00465-5

43. Kaewpradit, K., Ngamchaliew, P., & Buathong, N. (2025). Digital screen time usage, prevalence of excessive digital screen time, and its association with mental health, sleep quality, and academic performance among Southern University students.

Frontiers in Psychiatry, 16, Article 1535631.
https://doi.org/10.3389/fpsyt.2025.1535631

44. Kaur, N., Gupta, M., Chakrapani, V., Khan, F., Malhi, P., Kiran, T., & Grover, S. (2024). Effectiveness of a program to lower unwanted media screens among 2-5-year-old children: A randomized controlled trial. *Frontiers in Public Health, 12*, Article 1304861.
https://doi.org/10.3389/fpubh.2024.1304861

45. Kitching, E., Mullen, P. R., Chae, N., & Backer, A. (2024). School counselors' experiences of induction and mentoring. *Professional School Counseling, 28*(1), Article 2156759X241290492.
https://doi.org/10.1177/2156759X241290492

46. Larberg, J. L., & Sherlin, L. H. (2021). Grit and growth mindset contribution to school counseling services. *SAGE Open, 11*(2), Article 21582440211014512.
https://doi.org/10.1177/21582440211014512

47. Lin, H., Wang, Y., He, G., Li, J., & Zheng, H. (2025). The effect of school-based group counseling on Chinese mainland adolescents' mental health and academic functioning: A meta-analysis of controlled studies. *Journal of Counseling Psychology, 72*(4), 416–431.
https://doi.org/10.1037/cou0000789

48. Lastname, F. M. (Year). *Title of thesis in sentence case* (Publication No. ####) [Master's thesis, Indiana State University]. Indiana State University ScholarWorks.
https://scholars.indianastate.edu/cgi/viewcontent.cgi?article=2791&context=etds

49. Mahmood, A., Kedia, S., Arshad, H., Mou, X., & Dillon, P. J. (2024). Disparities in access to mental health services among children diagnosed with anxiety and depression in the United States. *Community Mental Health Journal, 60*(8), 1532-1546. https://doi.org/10.1007/s10597-024-01305-3

50. Martinez, R. R., Williams, R. G., & Green, J. (2020). The role of school counselors delivering a trauma-informed care approach to supporting youth in foster care. *Professional School Counseling, 23*(1), Article 10. https://doi.org/10.1177/2156759X20947747

51. Merlin-Knoblich, C., Graham, B., Clark, S., Song, S., & Harper, S. (2025). An exploration of the impact of the School Counseling Equity Fellowship on school counselors. *Journal of Counseling & Development*. Advance online publication. https://doi.org/10.1002/jcad.12566

52. Misra, S., Jackson, V. W., Chong, J., Choe, K., Tay, C., Wong, J., & Yang, L. H. (2021). Systematic review of cultural aspects of stigma and mental illness among racial and ethnic minority groups in the United States: Implications for interventions. *American Journal of Community Psychology, 68*(3–4), 486–512. https://doi.org/10.1002/ajcp.12516

53. Muhammad, R. (2024). The effectiveness of technology to improve educational counseling services: A systematic literature review. *Journal of Teaching and Learning, 18*(2), 111–127. https://doi.org/10.22329/jtl.v18i2.8709

54. Mullen, P. R., Chae, N., Backer, A., & Niles, J. (2021). School Counselor Burnout, Job Stress, and Job Satisfaction by Student

Caseload. *NASSP Bulletin, 105*(1), 25–42. https://doi.org/10.1177/0192636521999828

55. Nazari, A., Hosseinnia, M., & Torkian, S., et al. (2023). Social media and mental health in students: A cross-sectional study during the COVID-19 pandemic. *BMC Psychiatry, 23*, Article 458. https://doi.org/10.1186/s12888-023-04859-w

56. O'Dea, B., King, C., Subotic-Kerry, M., O'Moore, K., & Christensen, H. (2017). School counselors' perspectives of a web-based stepped care mental health service for schools: Cross-sectional online survey. *JMIR Mental Health, 4*(4), Article e55. https://doi.org/10.2196/mental.8369

57. Palmer, L. E., & Erford, B. T. (2012). Predicting student outcome measures using the ASCA National Model program audit. *The Professional Counselor, 2*(2), 152–159. https://doi.org/10.15241/lep.2.2.152

58. Panchal, N., Cox, C., & Rudowitz, R. (2025, September 11). The landscape of school-based mental health services [Issue brief]. KFF. Retrieved from https://www.kff.org/mental-health/the-landscape-of-school-based-mental-health-services/

59. Parzych, J. L., Generali, M., & Yavuz, O. (2021). School counseling programs identifying academic development needs: Student, parent, and faculty perceptions of academic needs and related services. *Journal of Education, 203*(1), 57–67. https://doi.org/10.1177/00220574211016433

60. Partain, C., & Goodwin, A. (2025, May 13). Most HISD schools don't have enough counselors. How could that impact college readiness goals? *Houston Chronicle*.

https://www.houstonchronicle.com/news/houston-
texas/education/hisd/article/counselors-hisd-ccmr-
20237953.php

61. Perryman, K. L., Timothy, T. J., & Frost, H. T. (2025). The
    school counselor's role in supporting teachers working with
    children who have experienced trauma: Lessons learned.
    Journal of Child & Adolescent Trauma, 18(2), 265-278.
    https://doi.org/10.1007/s40653-024-00680-z

62. Plackett, R., Blyth, A., & Schartau, P. (2023). The impact of
    social media use interventions on mental well-being: Systematic
    review. *Journal of Medical Internet Research, 25*, e44922.
    https://doi.org/10.2196/44922

63. Premachandran, P. (n.d.). Social-emotional learning integration
    across curriculum: Evidence-based practices and assessment
    frameworks. *International Journal of Educational Psychology*.
    Retrieved from
    https://eduresearchjournal.com/index.php/ijep/article/view/1
    36/117

64. PsyWellPath. (n.d.). History of school counseling. In
    PsyWellPath Glossary. Retrieved July 14, 2025, from
    https://glossary.psywellpath.com/history-of-school-
    counseling?utm

65. Reese, D. M. (2021). School counselor preparation to support
    inclusivity, equity and access for students of color with
    disabilities. *Frontiers in Education, 6*, Article 588528.
    https://doi.org/10.3389/feduc.2021.588528

66. Savitz Romer, M., & Nicola, T. P. (2022, January). *Building high-quality school counseling programs to ensure student success* (Brief No. 21). EdResearch for Recovery, Annenberg Institute at Brown University. https://edresearchforaction.org/research-briefs/building-high-quality-school-counseling-programs-to-ensure-student-success/

67. Simbolon, R., & Purba, W. (2022). Evaluating the impact of school counseling programs on student well-being and academic performance in the educational environment. *Jurnal Ilmu Pendidikan dan Humaniora, 11*(2), 118–137. https://doi.org/10.35335/jiph.v11i2.19

68. Steen, S., Melfie, J., Carro, A., & Shi, Q. (2022). A systematic literature review exploring achievement outcomes and therapeutic factors for group counseling interventions in schools. *Professional School Counseling, 26*(1a), 1–13. https://doi.org/10.1177/2156759X221086739

69. Syahrul, M., Rais, R., Yanti, Y., Prihatin, R., & Asni, Asni. (2025). The effect of emotional intelligence counseling on elementary school students' self-control in facing conflicts. *International Journal of Educatio Elementaria and Psychologia, 2*(1), 13–23. https://doi.org/10.70177/ijeep.v2i1.1881

70. Tucker, L. (2025, February 15). Strategic high school course selection: Necessary in competitive college admissions. *Dr. Tucker College Consultant*. Retrieved from https://drtucker.education/strategic-high-school-course-selection-necessary-in-competitive-college-admissions

71. University of South Australia. (2025, March 26). Study confirms that student wellbeing plays a critical role in academic success [News release]. AISL Mall. Retrieved from https://www.aislmall.com/news/study-confirms-wellbeing-plays-critical-role-in-academic-success/

72. Van Velsor, P. (2009). School counselors as social-emotional learning consultants: Where do we begin? *Professional School Counseling, 13*(1), 50–58. https://doi.org/10.5330/PSC.n.2010-13.50

73. Walker, L. J. (2018). Examining the Every Student Succeeds Act's impact on African American students' mental health access. *Teachers College Record, 120*(13), Article 016146811812001304. https://doi.org/10.1177/016146811812001304

74. Wang, D., & Wang, G. (2025). Improving career readiness in middle school students: A systematic review of intervention approaches. *Frontiers in Psychology, 16*, Article 1582195. https://doi.org/10.3389/fpsyg.2025.1582195

75. Warren, J. M., Blount, T. N., & Ricks, J. R. (2025). The use of implementation strategies in school counseling: A deductive qualitative analysis. *Professional School Counseling, 29*(1). https://doi.org/10.1177/2156759X251342491

76. World Health Organization. (2024, September 25). Teens, screens and mental health: New WHO report indicates need for healthier online habits among adolescents [Media release]. WHO Regional Office for Europe. Retrieved from https://www.who.int/europe/news/item/25-09-2024-teens--screens-and-mental-health

77. YouScience. (2025). *2025 School Counselor Report: The state of school counseling in America: Addressing challenges, celebrating successes, and expanding impact for all*. https://resources.youscience.com/rs/806-BFU-539/images/2025_SchoolCounselorReport.pdf

78. Zhu, Y., Chen, H., Li, J., Mei, X., & Wang, W. (2023). Effects of different interventions on internet addiction: A systematic review and network meta-analysis. *BMC Psychiatry, 23*(1), Article 921. https://doi.org/10.1186/s12888-023-05400-9

About the Author

Dr. Wladimir Lewis-Thomas is a former school counselor and administrator with a career spanning more than three decades in both private and public school settings. After retiring from public education, he continues to guide and inspire future professionals as a graduate-level instructor. He also serves as Assistant Director for Political and External Affairs for the Council of School Supervisors and Administrators (CSA), representing school leaders across New York City.

A devoted Episcopalian, Dr. Lewis-Thomas is an active member of St. Ann & the Holy Trinity – the Pro-Cathedral of the Episcopal Diocese of Long Island, where he volunteers and serves as a Lay Eucharistic Minister.

Outside of his professional and faith commitments, he is a passionate singer, an avid traveler, and a lifelong admirer of Haitian music and cuisine. Above all, he values time spent with his family and loved ones, who remain the foundation of his inspiration and joy.

www.ingramcontent.com/pod-product-compliance
Lightning Source LLC
Chambersburg PA
CBHW071753120626
46550CB00002B/778